JUSTICE LEAGUE OF AMERICA
THE INJUSTICE LEAGUE

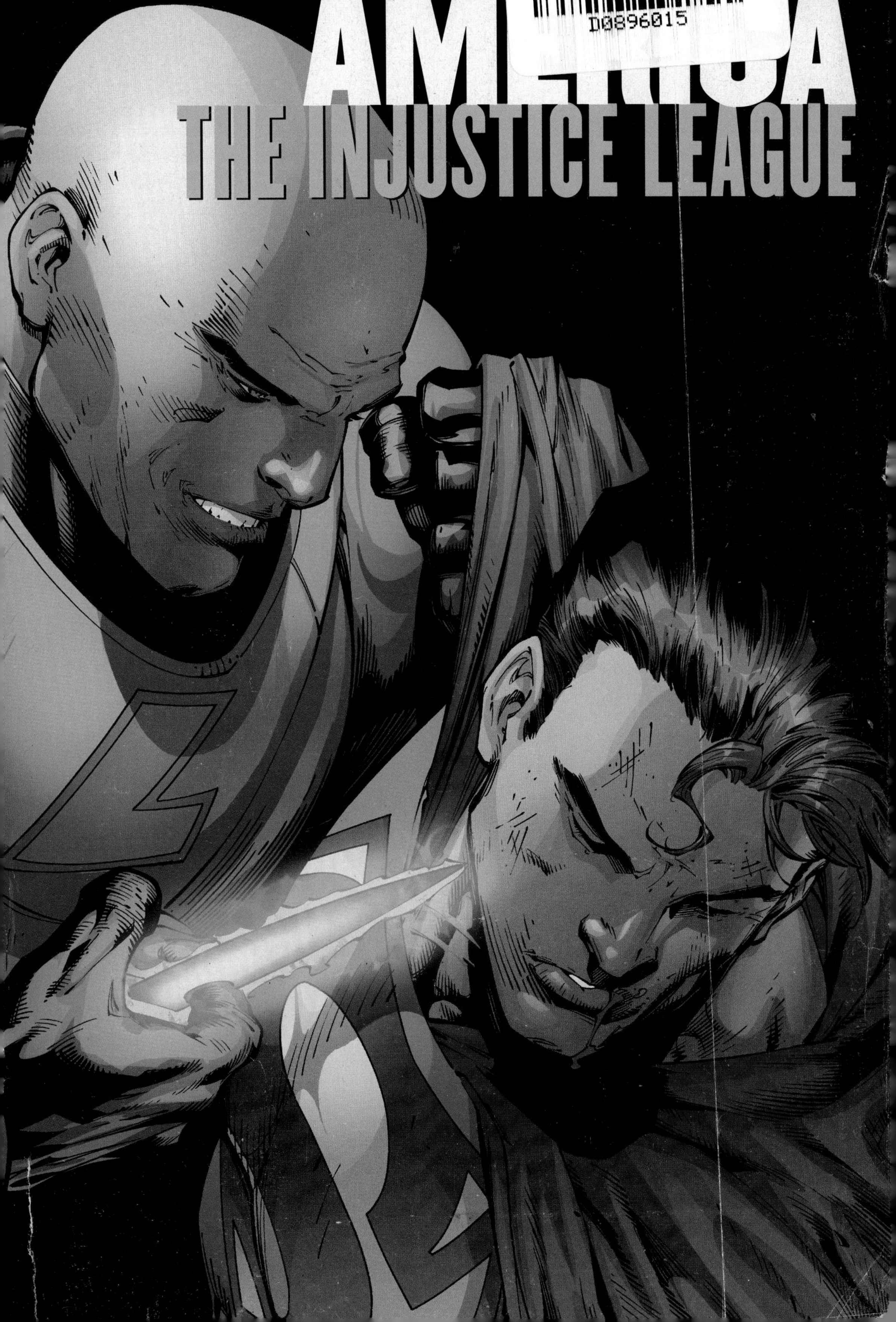

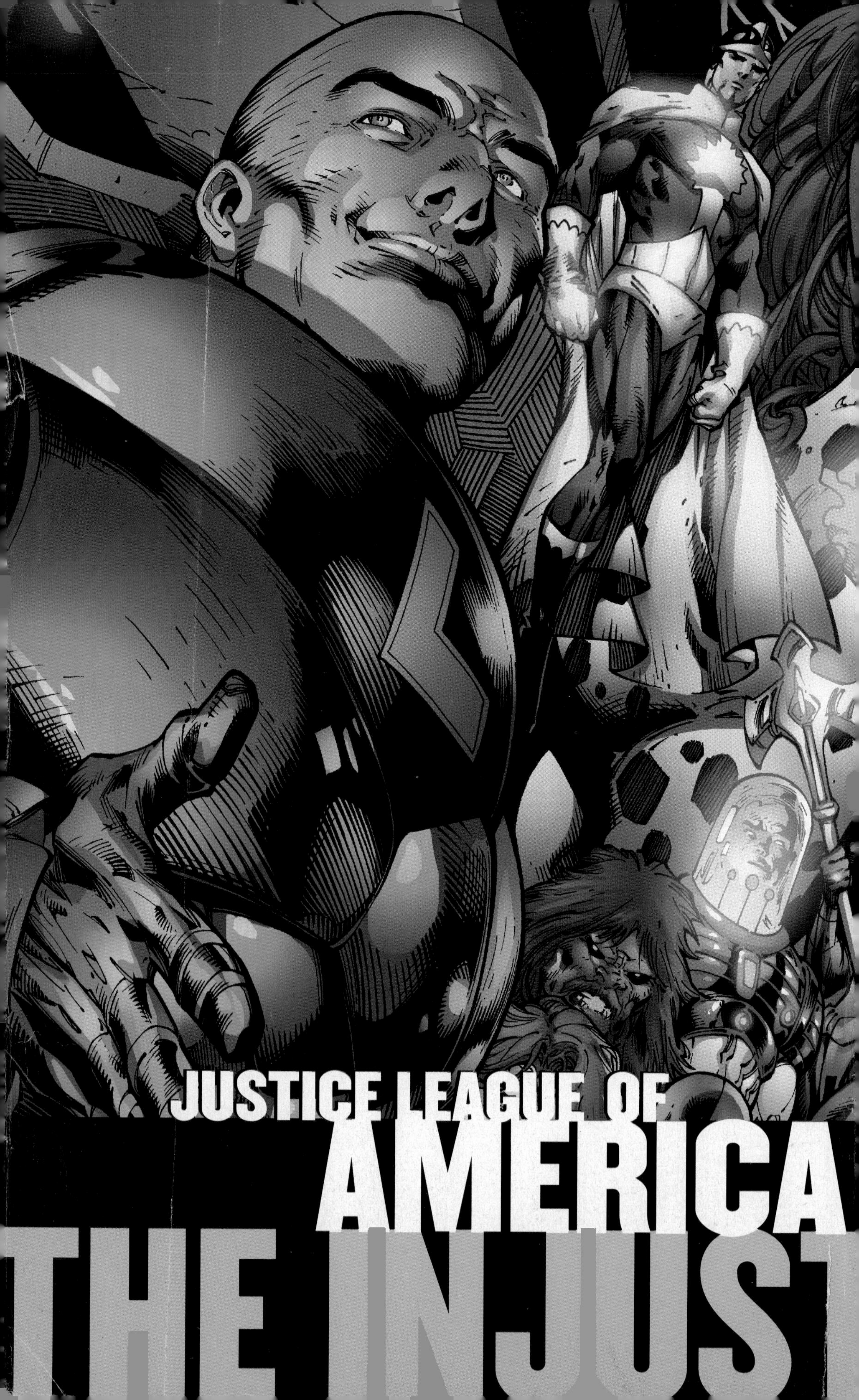
JUSTICE LEAGUE OF
AMERICA
THE INJUST

Dwayne McDuffie Writer

The Injustice League

Chapter 1
Mike McKone Penciller
Andy Lanning Inker

Chapter 2
Joe Benitez Penciller
Victor Llamas Inker

Chapters 3 + 4
Ed Benes Penciller
Sandra Hope Inker

A Brief Tangent

Joe Benitez Penciller
Victor Llamas Inker

Soup Kitchen

Alan Burnett Writer
Allan Jefferson Artist

Pete Pantazis
Alex Sinclair Colorists

Rob Leigh Letterer

ICE LEAGUE

Cover by **Ian Churchill & Norm Rapmund**
with **Alex Sinclair**
Logo designed by **Ken Lopez**

Justice League of America: The Injustice League

DC Comics, 1700 Broadway, New York, NY 10019
A Warner Bros. Entertainment Company
Printed in Canada. First Printing.

HC ISBN: 978-1-4012-1802-7
SC ISBN: 978-1-4012-2050-1

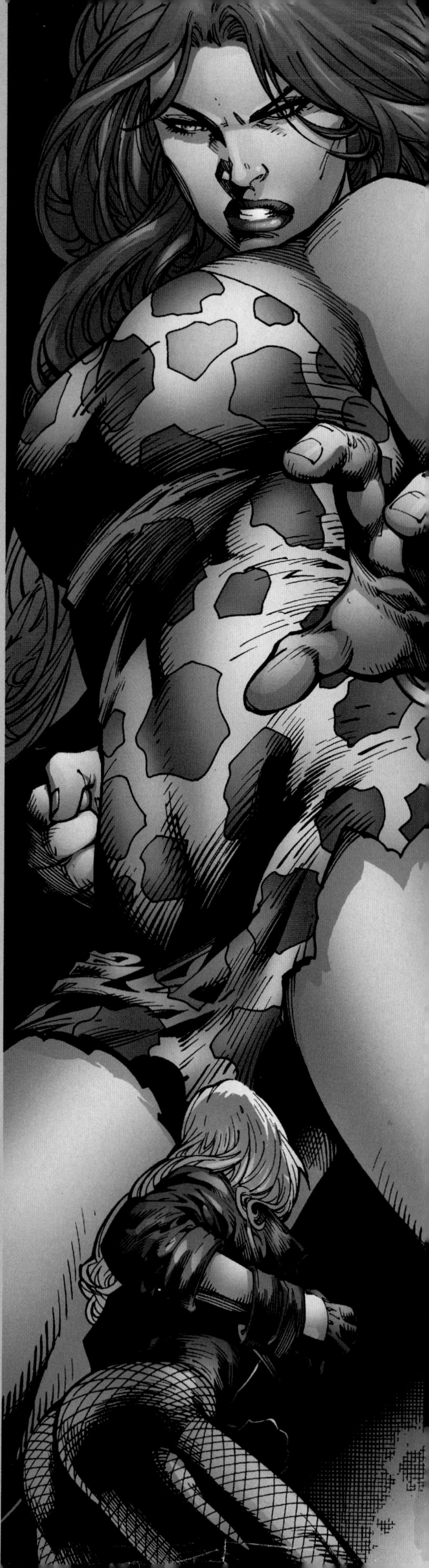

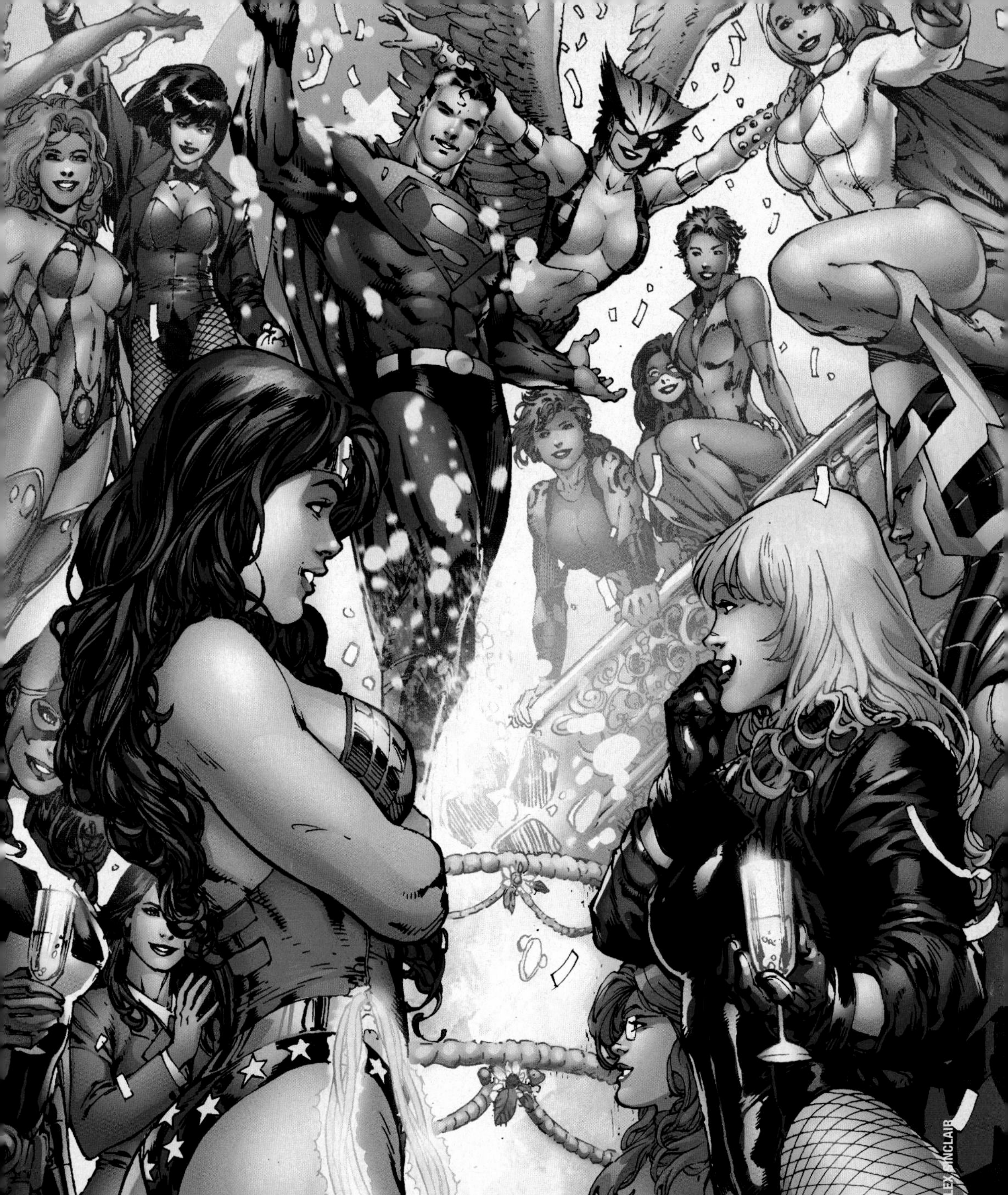
COVER ART BY ED BENES WITH ALEX SINCLAIR

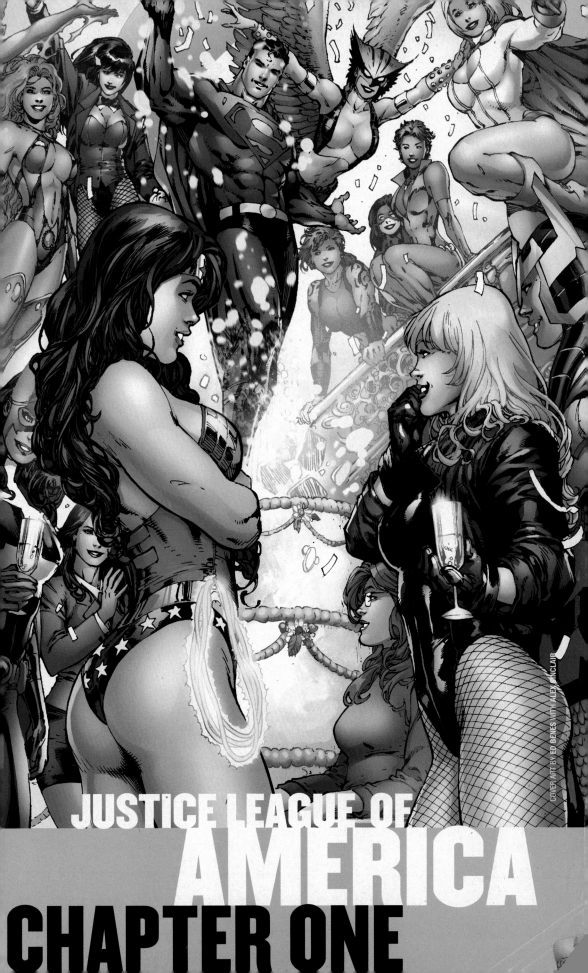

JUSTICE LEAGUE OF AMERICA

CHAPTER ONE

"Welcome to the Hall of Doom."

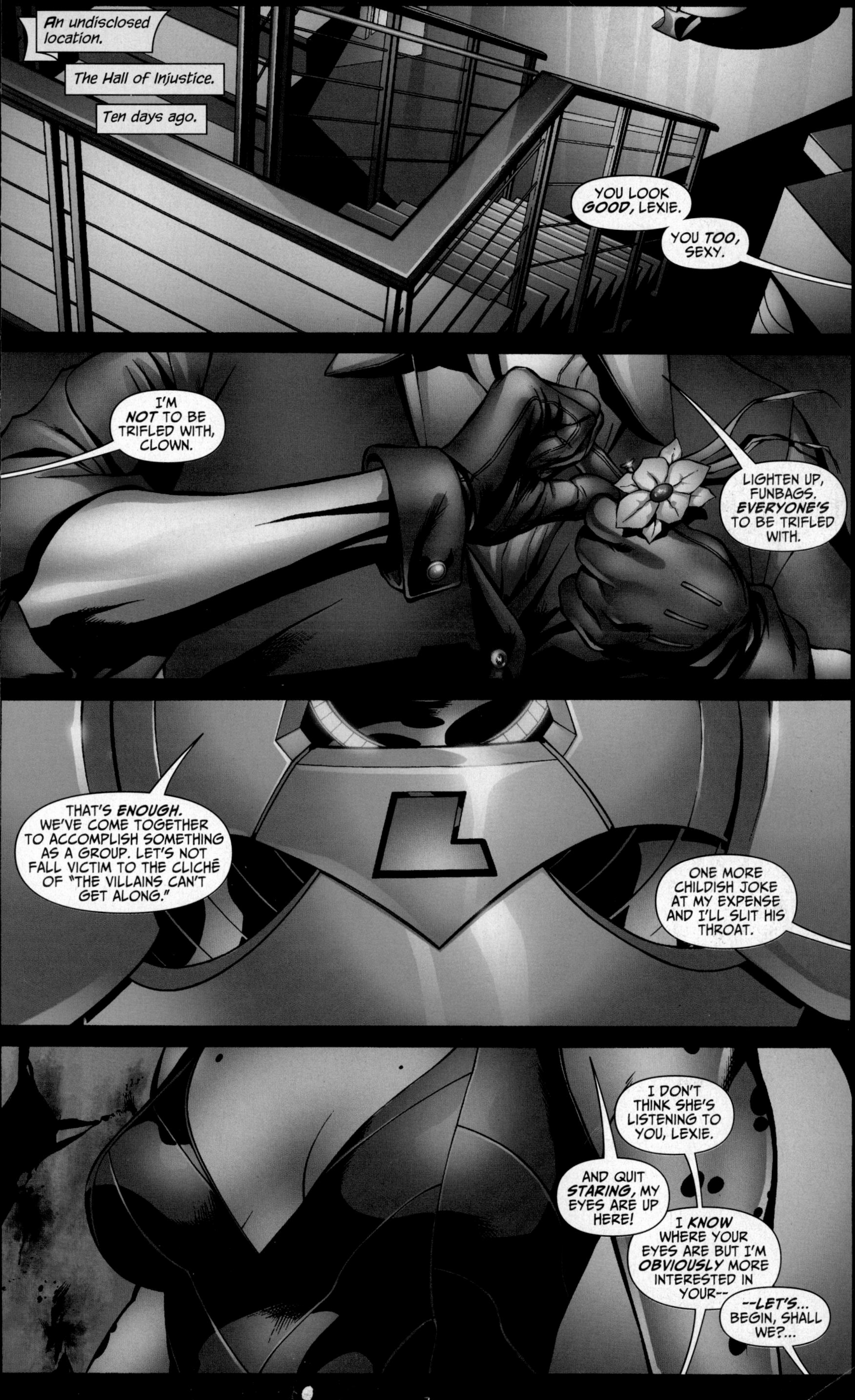
An undisclosed location.
The Hall of Injustice.
Ten days ago.
YOU LOOK GOOD, LEXIE.
YOU TOO, SEXY.
I'M NOT TO BE TRIFLED WITH, CLOWN.
LIGHTEN UP, FUNBAGS. EVERYONE'S TO BE TRIFLED WITH.
THAT'S ENOUGH. WE'VE COME TOGETHER TO ACCOMPLISH SOMETHING AS A GROUP. LET'S NOT FALL VICTIM TO THE CLICHÉ OF "THE VILLAINS CAN'T GET ALONG."
ONE MORE CHILDISH JOKE AT MY EXPENSE AND I'LL SLIT HIS THROAT.
I DON'T THINK SHE'S LISTENING TO YOU, LEXIE.
AND QUIT STARING, MY EYES ARE UP HERE!
I KNOW WHERE YOUR EYES ARE BUT I'M OBVIOUSLY MORE INTERESTED IN YOUR--
--LET'S... BEGIN, SHALL WE?...

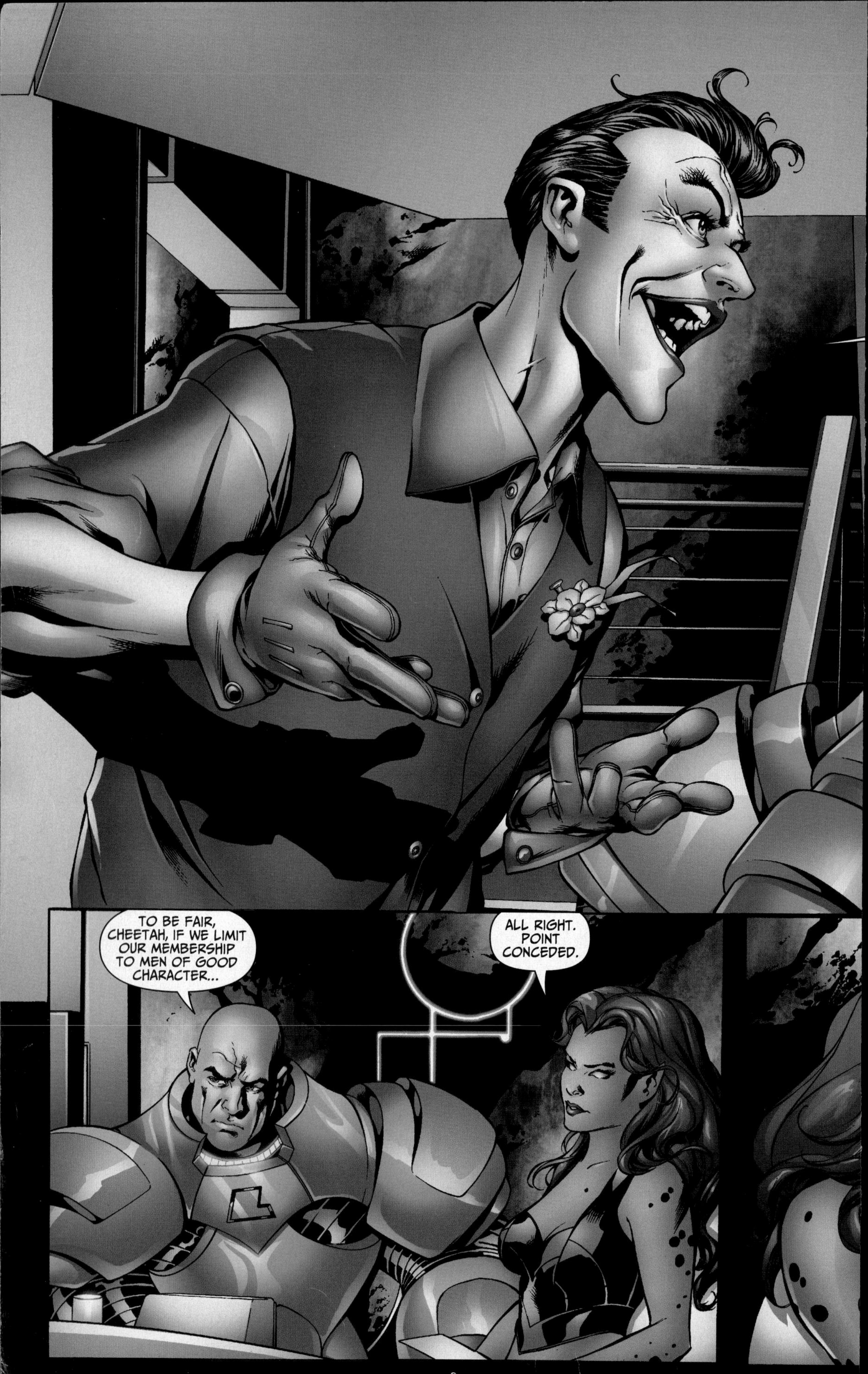
TO BE FAIR, CHEETAH, IF WE LIMIT OUR MEMBERSHIP TO MEN OF GOOD CHARACTER...
ALL RIGHT. POINT CONCEDED.

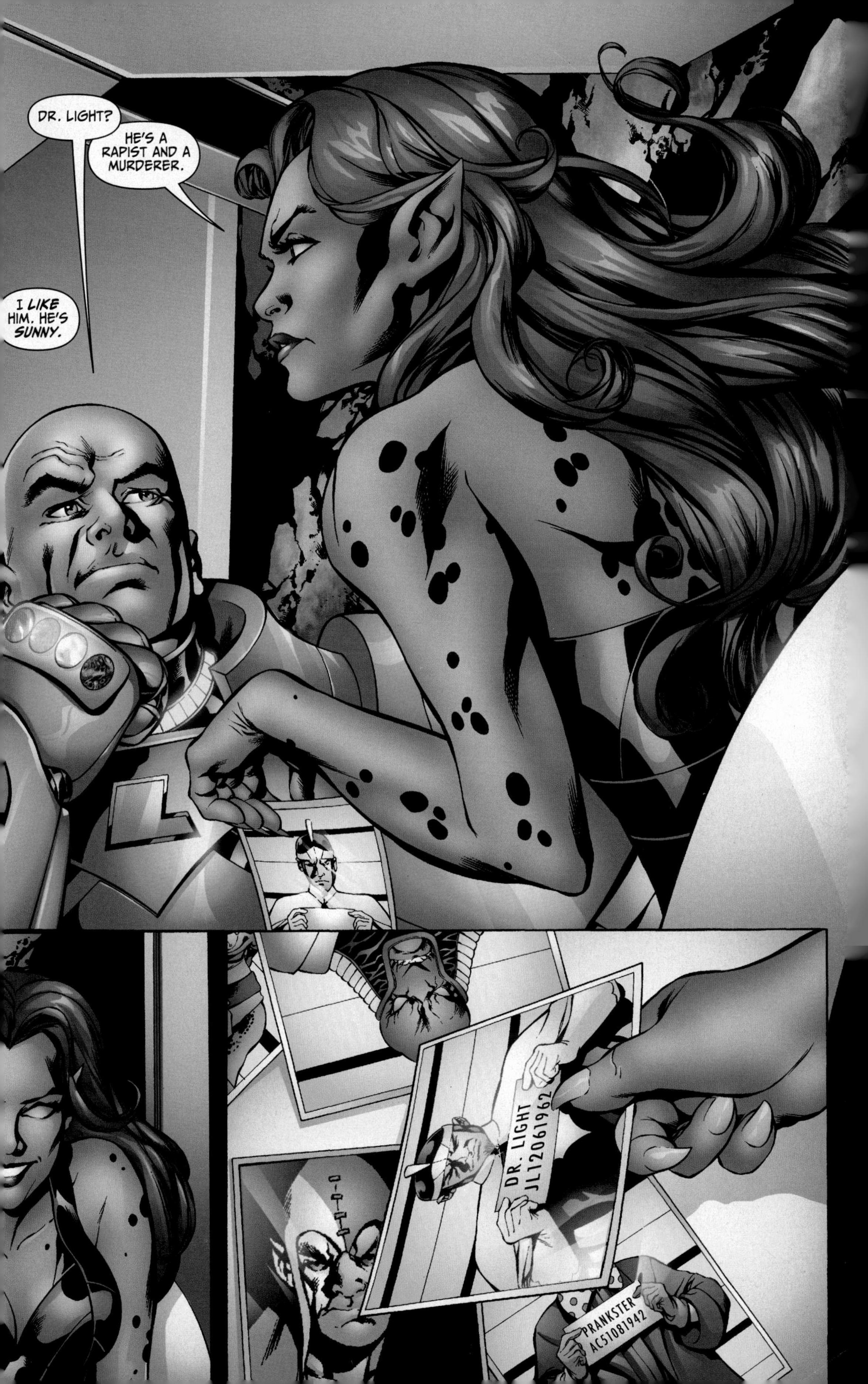
DR. LIGHT?
HE'S A RAPIST AND A MURDERER.
I LIKE HIM. HE'S SUNNY.
DR. LIGHT JL12061962
PRANKSTER AC51081942

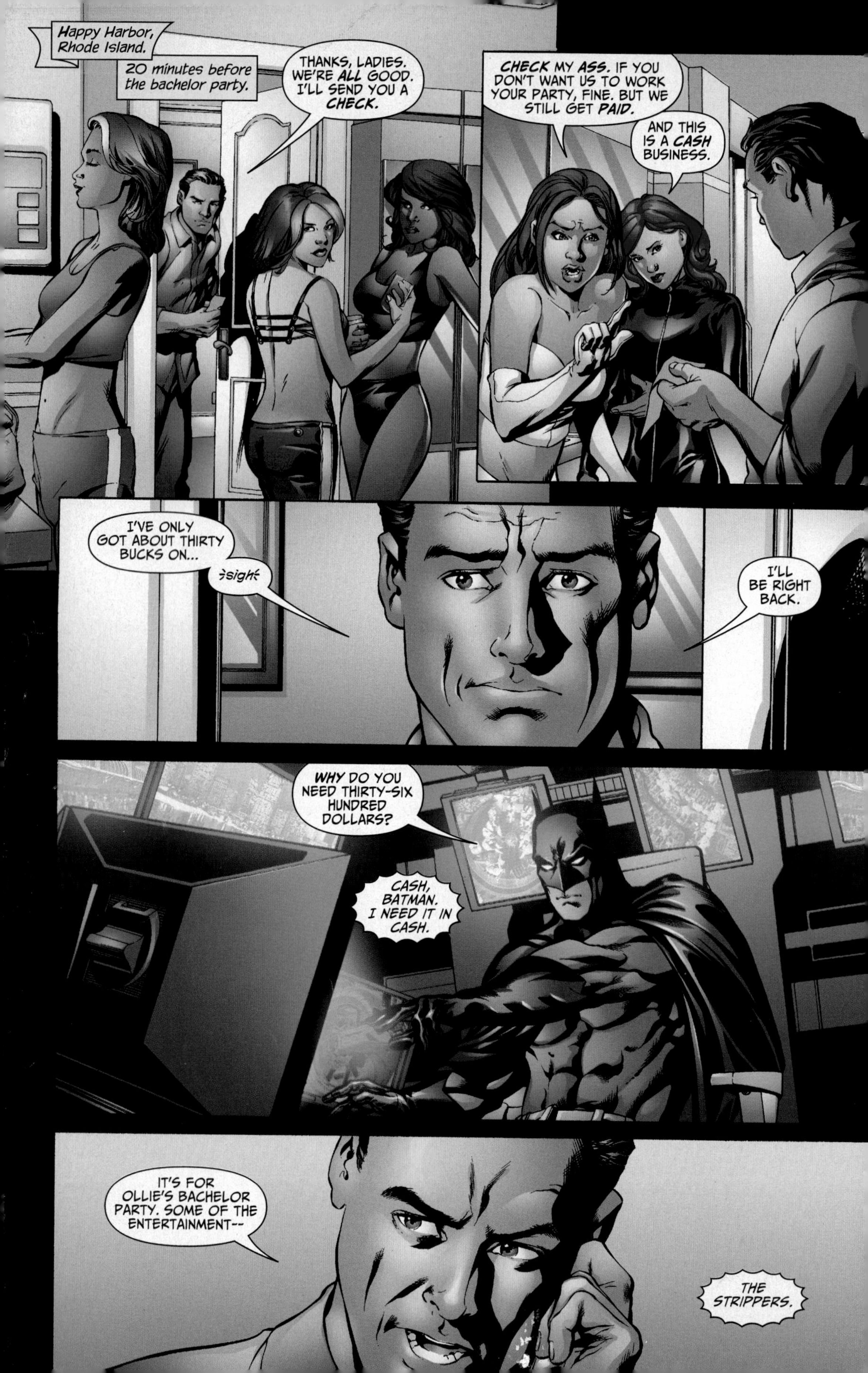

Happy Harbor, Rhode Island.
20 minutes before the bachelor party.
THANKS, LADIES. WE'RE ALL GOOD. I'LL SEND YOU A CHECK.
CHECK MY ASS. IF YOU DON'T WANT US TO WORK YOUR PARTY, FINE. BUT WE STILL GET PAID.
AND THIS IS A CASH BUSINESS.
I'VE ONLY GOT ABOUT THIRTY BUCKS ON...
sigh
I'LL BE RIGHT BACK.
WHY DO YOU NEED THIRTY-SIX HUNDRED DOLLARS?
CASH, BATMAN. I NEED IT IN CASH.
IT'S FOR OLLIE'S BACHELOR PARTY. SOME OF THE ENTERTAINMENT--
THE STRIPPERS.

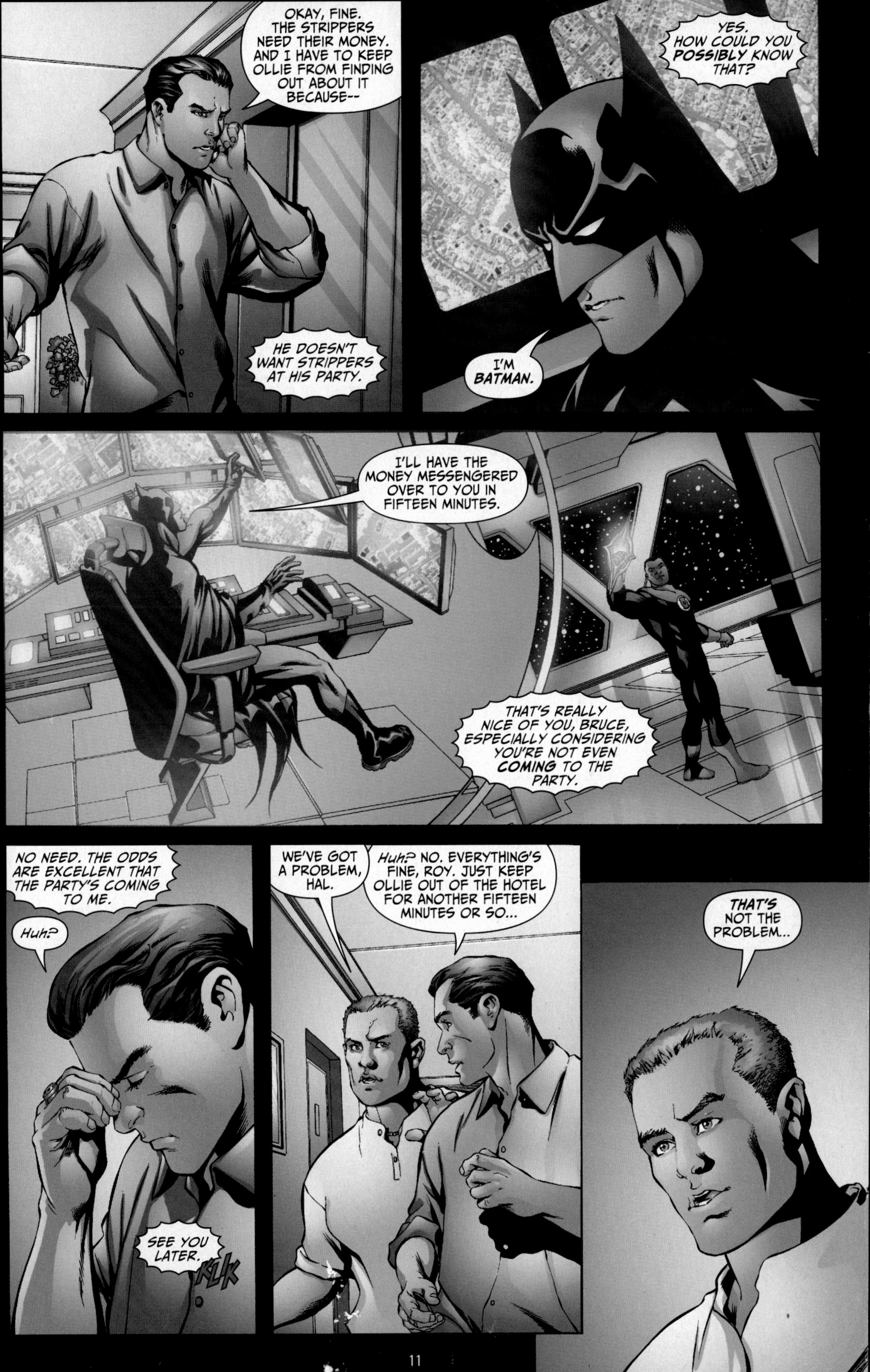
OKAY, FINE. THE STRIPPERS NEED THEIR MONEY. AND I HAVE TO KEEP OLLIE FROM FINDING OUT ABOUT IT BECAUSE--
HE DOESN'T WANT STRIPPERS AT HIS PARTY.
YES. HOW COULD YOU POSSIBLY KNOW THAT?
I'M BATMAN.
I'LL HAVE THE MONEY MESSENGERED OVER TO YOU IN FIFTEEN MINUTES.
THAT'S REALLY NICE OF YOU, BRUCE, ESPECIALLY CONSIDERING YOU'RE NOT EVEN COMING TO THE PARTY.
NO NEED. THE ODDS ARE EXCELLENT THAT THE PARTY'S COMING TO ME.
Huh?
SEE YOU LATER.
KLIK
WE'VE GOT A PROBLEM, HAL.
Huh? NO. EVERYTHING'S FINE, ROY. JUST KEEP OLLIE OUT OF THE HOTEL FOR ANOTHER FIFTEEN MINUTES OR SO...
THAT'S NOT THE PROBLEM...

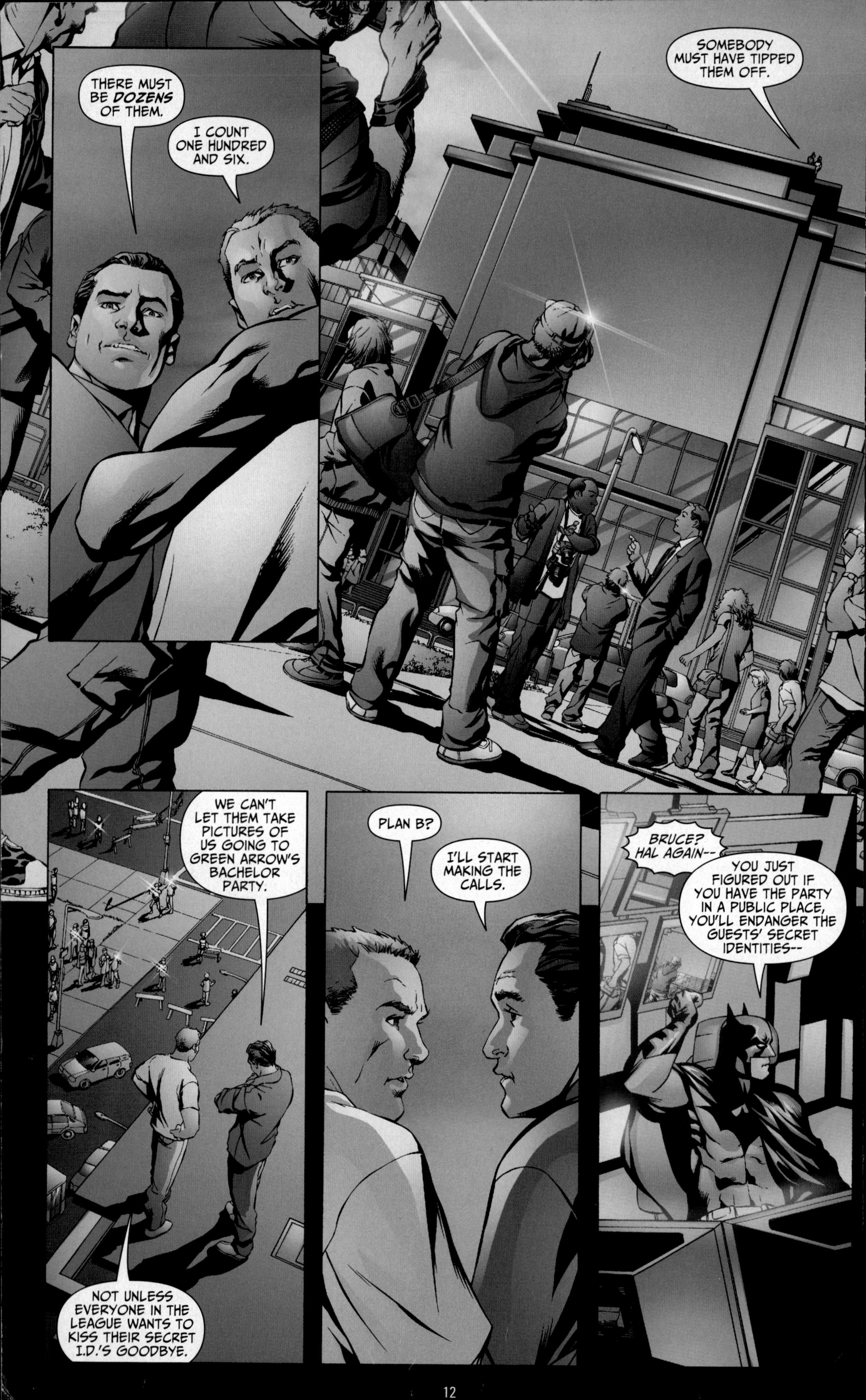
THERE MUST BE *DOZENS* OF THEM.
I COUNT ONE HUNDRED AND SIX.
SOMEBODY MUST HAVE TIPPED THEM OFF.
WE CAN'T LET THEM TAKE PICTURES OF US GOING TO GREEN ARROW'S BACHELOR PARTY.
NOT UNLESS EVERYONE IN THE LEAGUE WANTS TO KISS THEIR SECRET I.D.'S GOODBYE.
PLAN B?
I'LL START MAKING THE CALLS.
BRUCE? HAL AGAIN--
YOU JUST FIGURED OUT IF YOU HAVE THE PARTY IN A PUBLIC PLACE, YOU'LL ENDANGER THE GUESTS' SECRET IDENTITIES--

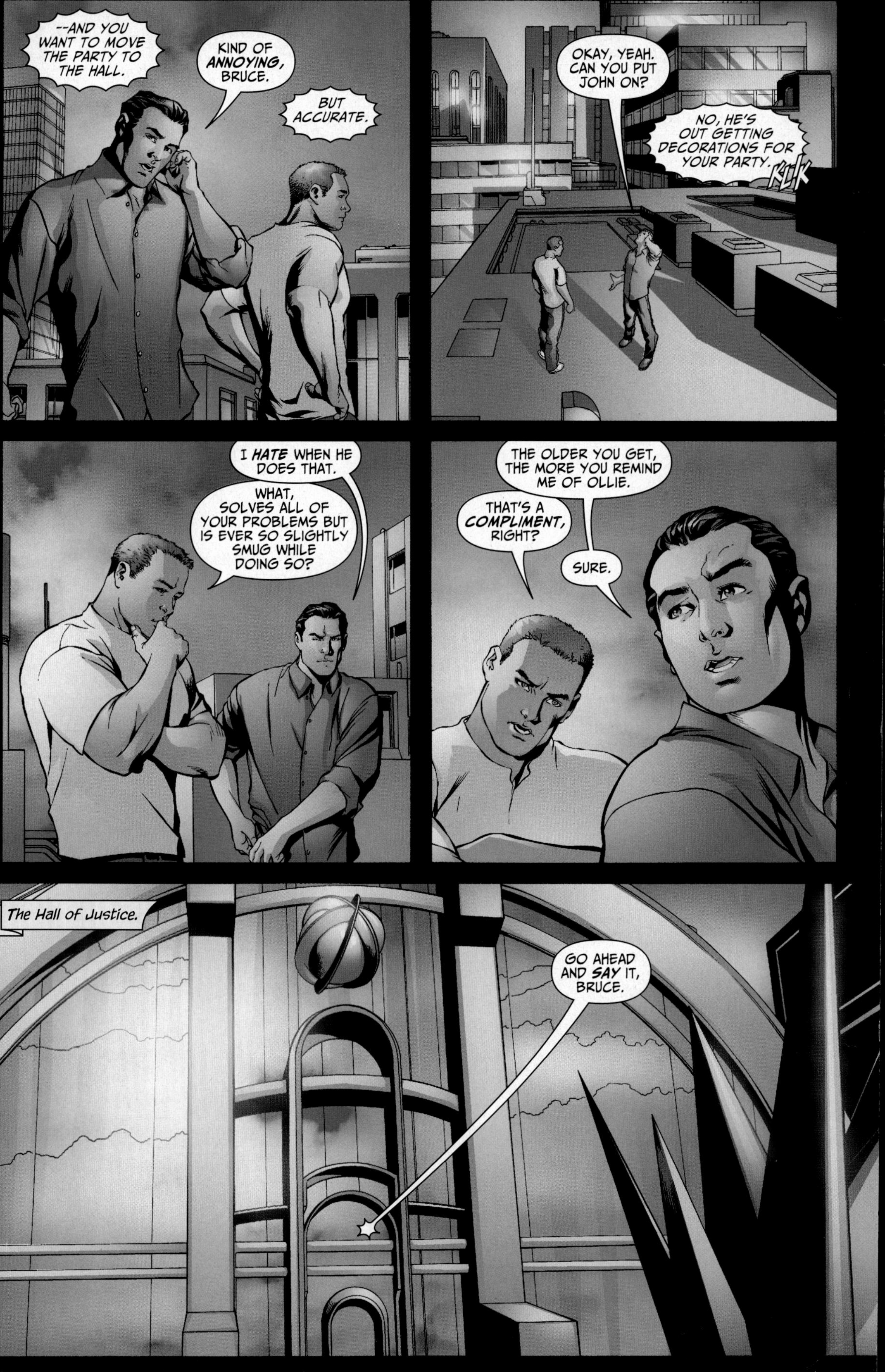
--AND YOU WANT TO MOVE THE PARTY TO THE HALL.
KIND OF ANNOYING, BRUCE.
BUT ACCURATE.
OKAY, YEAH. CAN YOU PUT JOHN ON?
NO, HE'S OUT GETTING DECORATIONS FOR YOUR PARTY.
KLIK
I HATE WHEN HE DOES THAT.
WHAT, SOLVES ALL OF YOUR PROBLEMS BUT IS EVER SO SLIGHTLY SMUG WHILE DOING SO?
THE OLDER YOU GET, THE MORE YOU REMIND ME OF OLLIE.
THAT'S A COMPLIMENT, RIGHT?
SURE.
The Hall of Justice.
GO AHEAD AND SAY IT, BRUCE.

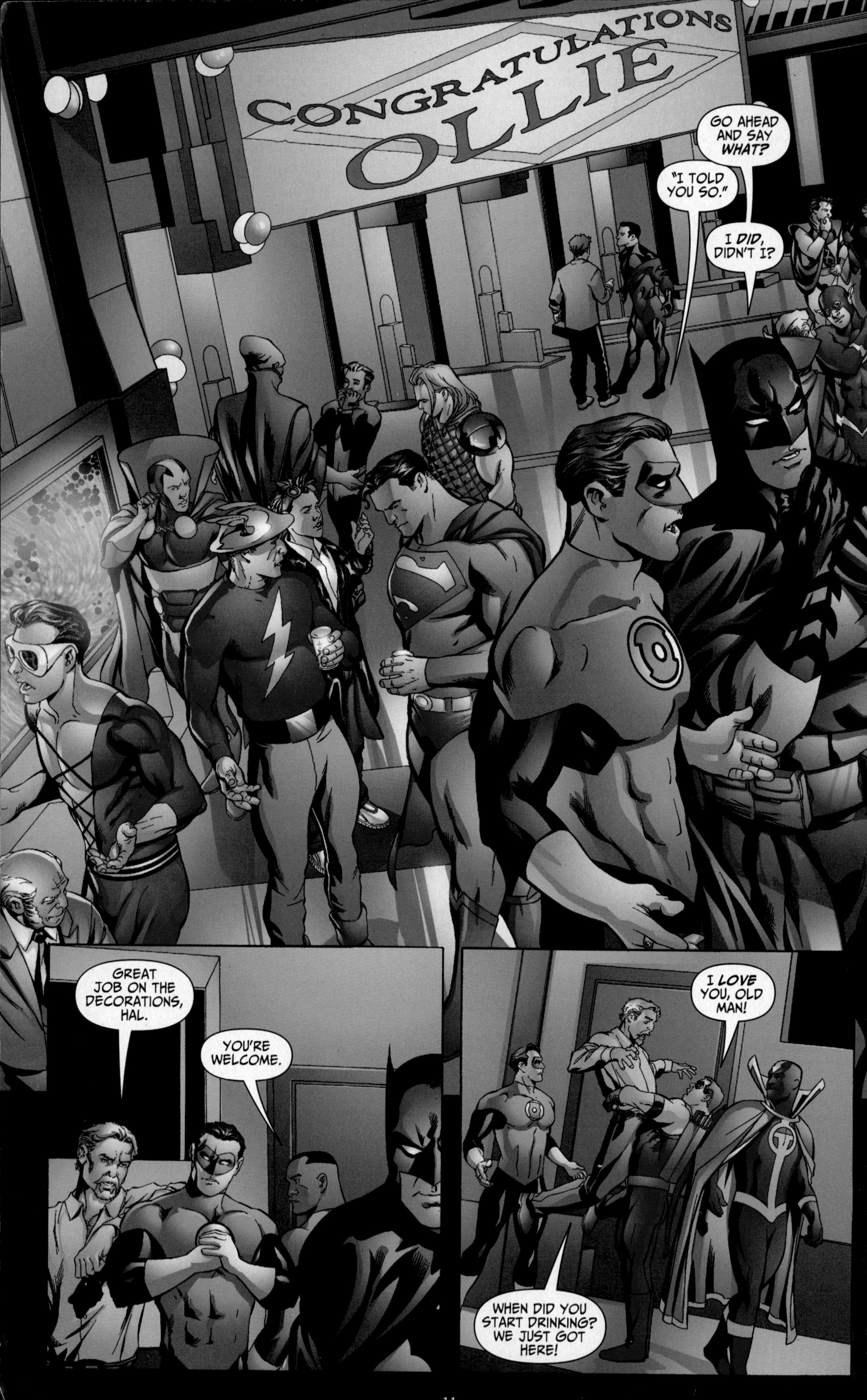
CONGRATULATIONS OLLIE
GO AHEAD AND SAY WHAT?
"I TOLD YOU SO."
I DID, DIDN'T I?
GREAT JOB ON THE DECORATIONS, HAL.
YOU'RE WELCOME.
I LOVE YOU, OLD MAN!
WHEN DID YOU START DRINKING? WE JUST GOT HERE!

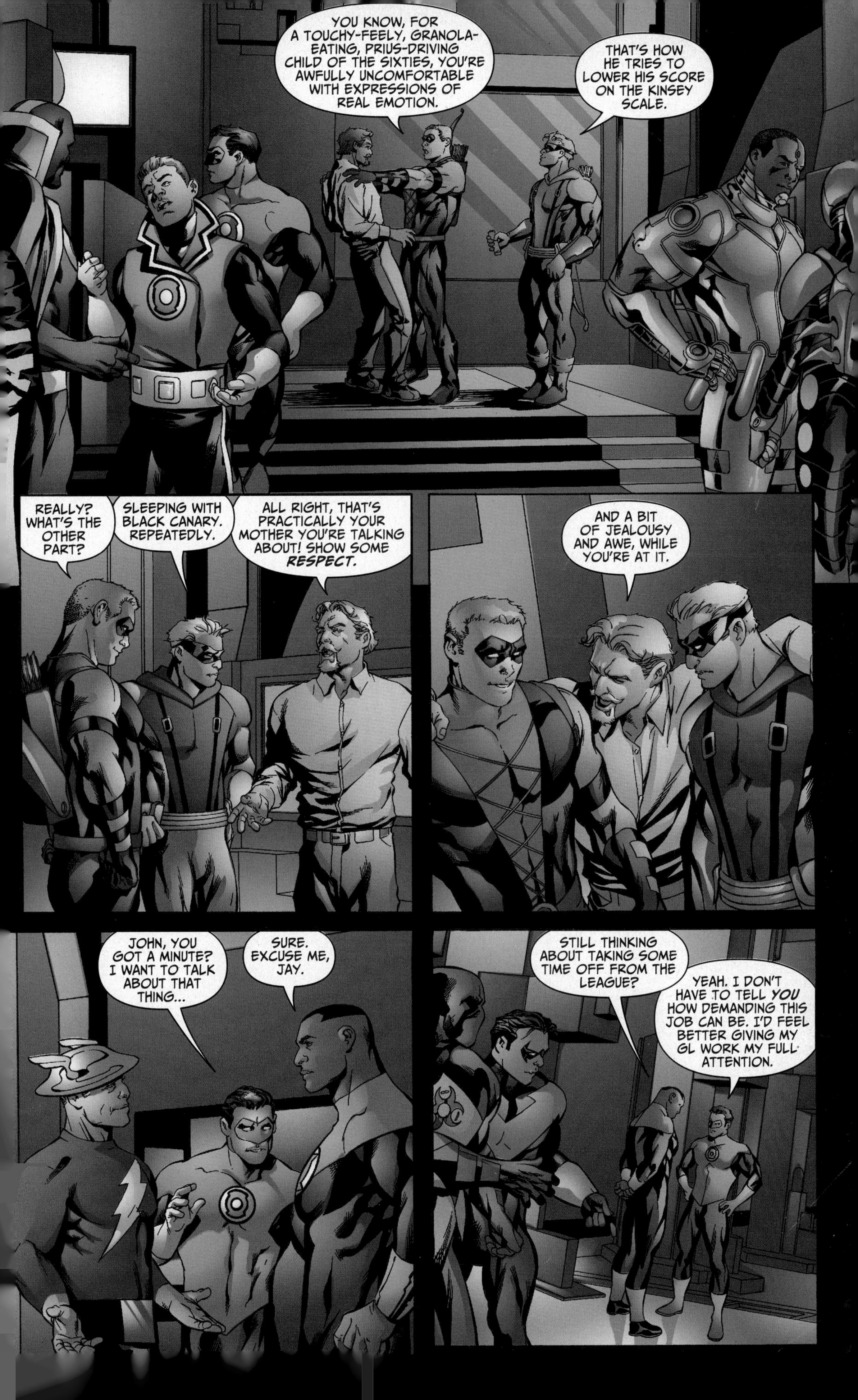
YOU KNOW, FOR A TOUCHY-FEELY, GRANOLA-EATING, PRIUS-DRIVING CHILD OF THE SIXTIES, YOU'RE AWFULLY UNCOMFORTABLE WITH EXPRESSIONS OF REAL EMOTION.
THAT'S HOW HE TRIES TO LOWER HIS SCORE ON THE KINSEY SCALE.
REALLY? WHAT'S THE OTHER PART?
SLEEPING WITH BLACK CANARY. REPEATEDLY.
ALL RIGHT, THAT'S PRACTICALLY YOUR MOTHER YOU'RE TALKING ABOUT! SHOW SOME *RESPECT.*
AND A BIT OF JEALOUSY AND AWE, WHILE YOU'RE AT IT.
JOHN, YOU GOT A MINUTE? I WANT TO TALK ABOUT THAT THING...
SURE. EXCUSE ME, JAY.
STILL THINKING ABOUT TAKING SOME TIME OFF FROM THE LEAGUE?
YEAH. I DON'T HAVE TO TELL *YOU* HOW DEMANDING THIS JOB CAN BE. I'D FEEL BETTER GIVING MY GL WORK MY FULL ATTENTION.

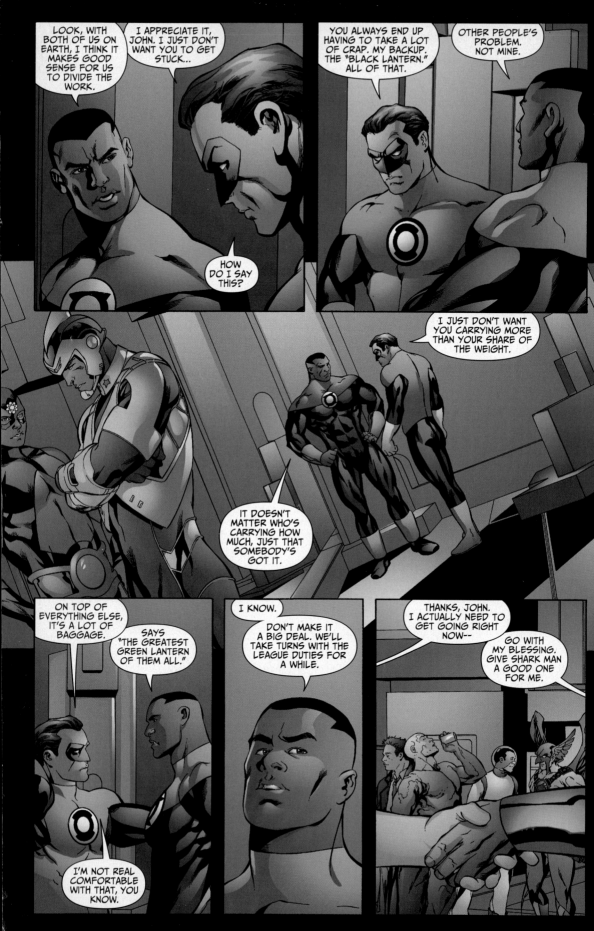

LOOK, WITH BOTH OF US ON EARTH, I THINK IT MAKES GOOD SENSE FOR US TO DIVIDE THE WORK.

I APPRECIATE IT, JOHN. I JUST DON'T WANT YOU TO GET STUCK...

YOU ALWAYS END UP HAVING TO TAKE A LOT OF CRAP. MY BACKUP. THE "BLACK LANTERN." ALL OF THAT.

OTHER PEOPLE'S PROBLEM. NOT MINE.

HOW DO I SAY THIS?

I JUST DON'T WANT YOU CARRYING MORE THAN YOUR SHARE OF THE WEIGHT.

IT DOESN'T MATTER WHO'S CARRYING HOW MUCH, JUST THAT SOMEBODY'S GOT IT.

ON TOP OF EVERYTHING ELSE, IT'S A LOT OF BAGGAGE.

SAYS "THE GREATEST GREEN LANTERN OF THEM ALL."

I KNOW.

DON'T MAKE IT A BIG DEAL. WE'LL TAKE TURNS WITH THE LEAGUE DUTIES FOR A WHILE.

THANKS, JOHN. I ACTUALLY NEED TO GET GOING RIGHT NOW--

GO WITH MY BLESSING. GIVE SHARK MAN A GOOD ONE FOR ME.

I'M NOT REAL COMFORTABLE WITH THAT, YOU KNOW.

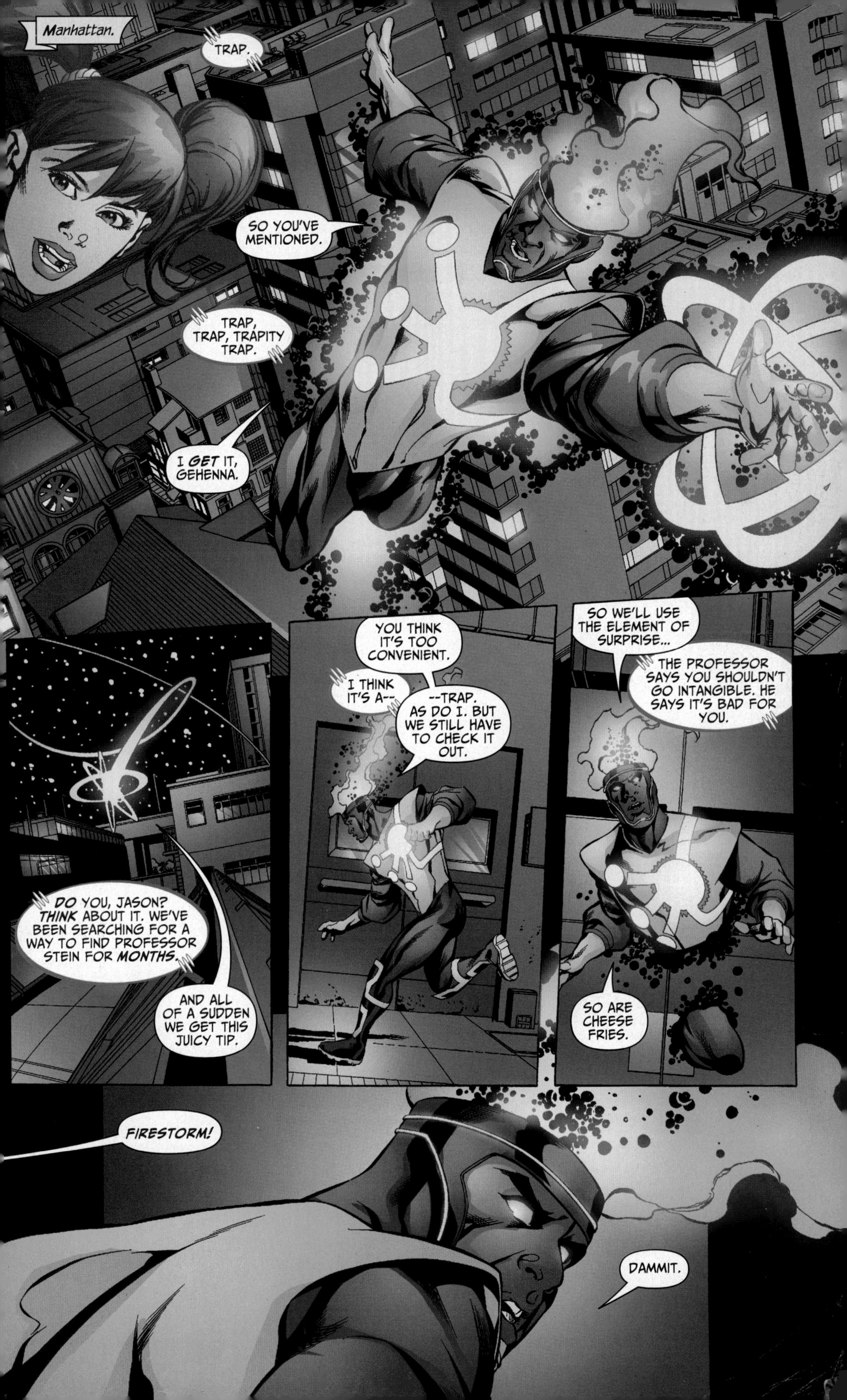
Manhattan.
TRAP.
SO YOU'VE MENTIONED.
TRAP, TRAP, TRAPITY TRAP.
I GET IT, GEHENNA.
DO YOU, JASON? THINK ABOUT IT. WE'VE BEEN SEARCHING FOR A WAY TO FIND PROFESSOR STEIN FOR MONTHS.
AND ALL OF A SUDDEN WE GET THIS JUICY TIP.
YOU THINK IT'S TOO CONVENIENT.
I THINK IT'S A--
--TRAP. AS DO I. BUT WE STILL HAVE TO CHECK IT OUT.
SO WE'LL USE THE ELEMENT OF SURPRISE...
THE PROFESSOR SAYS YOU SHOULDN'T GO INTANGIBLE. HE SAYS IT'S BAD FOR YOU.
SO ARE CHEESE FRIES.
FIRESTORM!
DAMMIT.

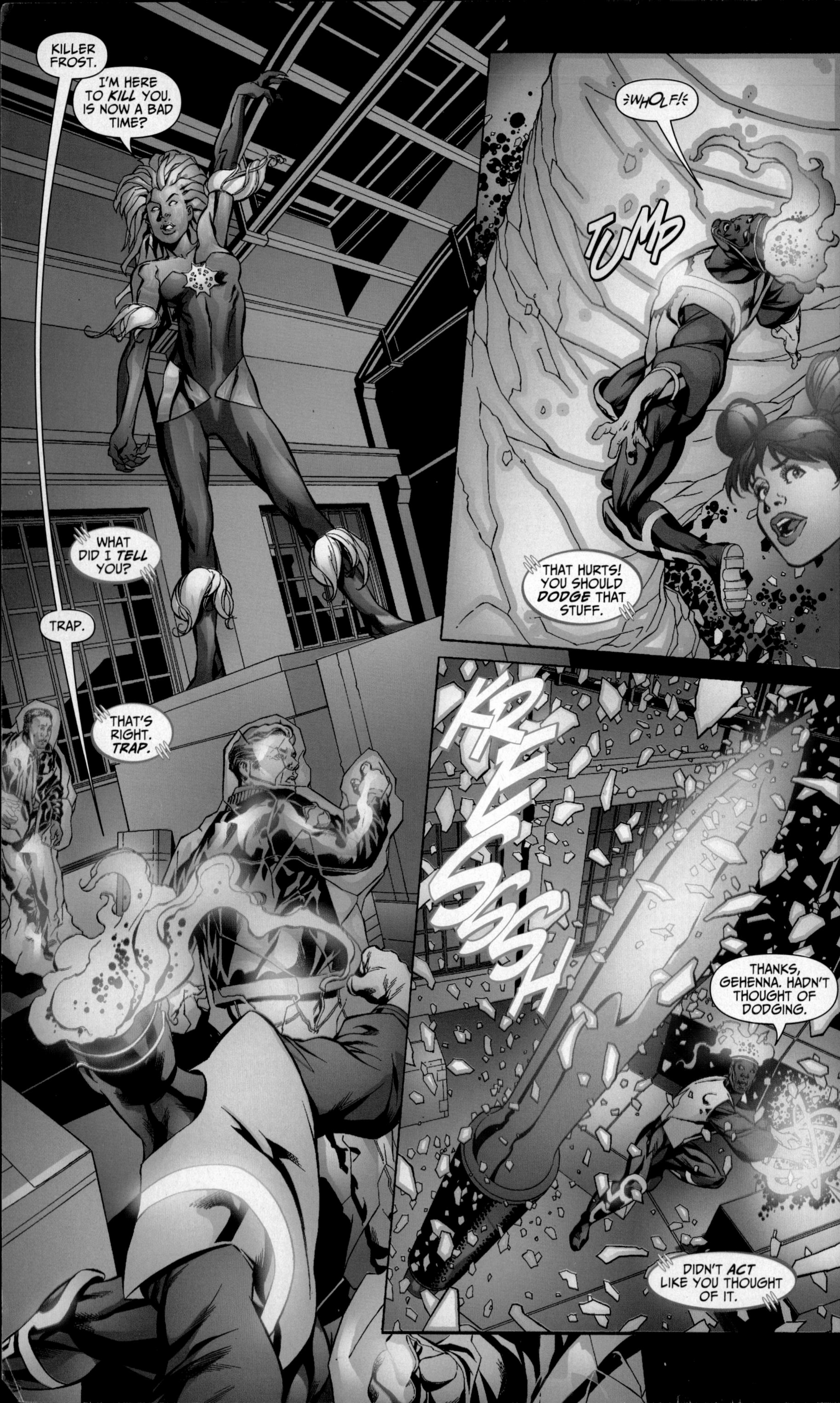

KILLER FROST.
I'M HERE TO KILL YOU. IS NOW A BAD TIME?
WHAT DID I TELL YOU?
TRAP.
THAT'S RIGHT. TRAP.
WHOLF!
TUMP
THAT HURTS! YOU SHOULD DODGE THAT STUFF.
KRRSSSSH
THANKS, GEHENNA. HADN'T THOUGHT OF DODGING.
DIDN'T ACT LIKE YOU THOUGHT OF IT.

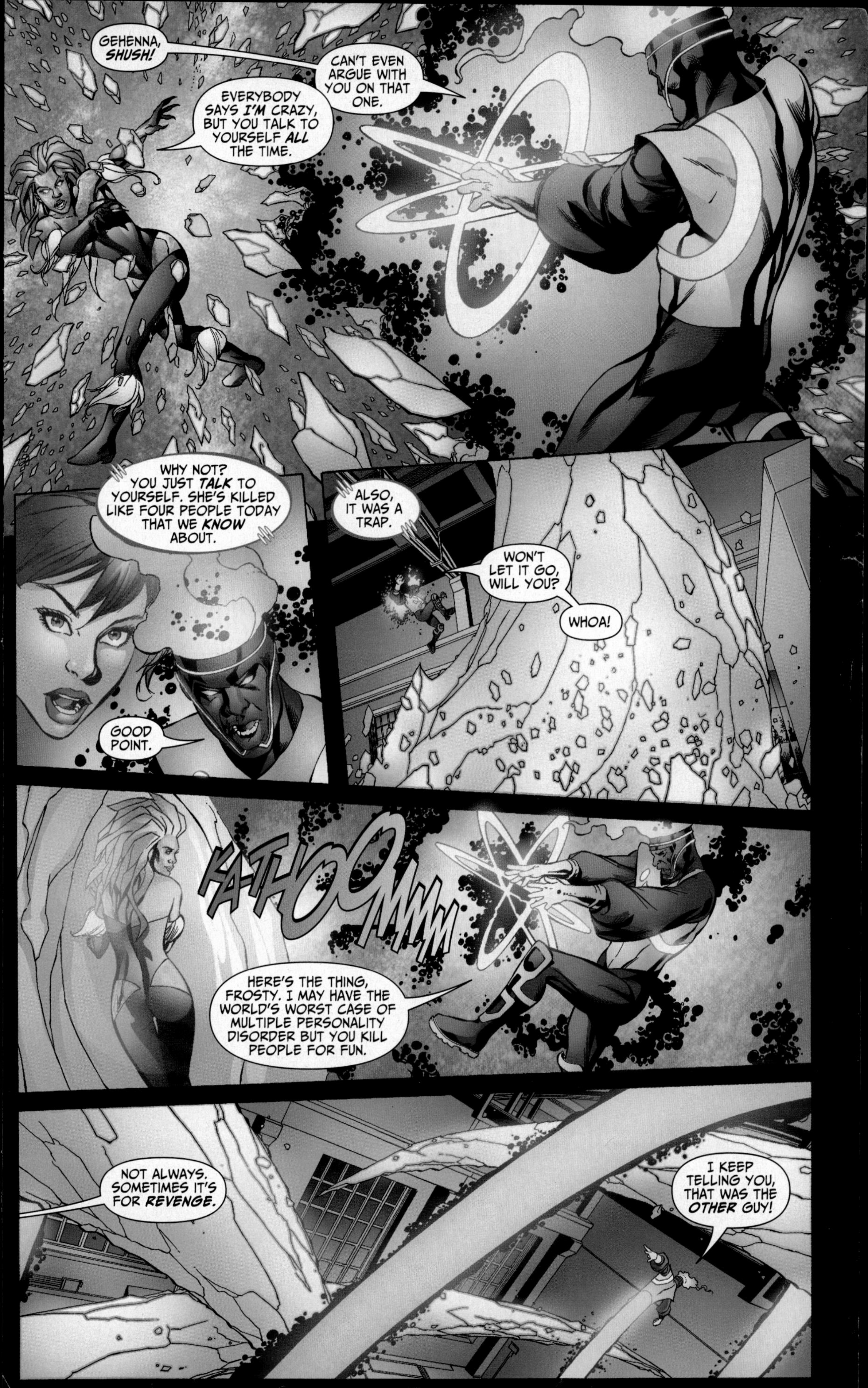
GEHENNA, SHUSH!
CAN'T EVEN ARGUE WITH YOU ON THAT ONE.
EVERYBODY SAYS I'M CRAZY, BUT YOU TALK TO YOURSELF ALL THE TIME.
WHY NOT? YOU JUST TALK TO YOURSELF. SHE'S KILLED LIKE FOUR PEOPLE TODAY THAT WE KNOW ABOUT.
GOOD POINT.
ALSO, IT WAS A TRAP.
WON'T LET IT GO, WILL YOU?
WHOA!
KA-THOOMMMM
HERE'S THE THING, FROSTY. I MAY HAVE THE WORLD'S WORST CASE OF MULTIPLE PERSONALITY DISORDER BUT YOU KILL PEOPLE FOR FUN.
NOT ALWAYS. SOMETIMES IT'S FOR REVENGE.
I KEEP TELLING YOU, THAT WAS THE OTHER GUY!

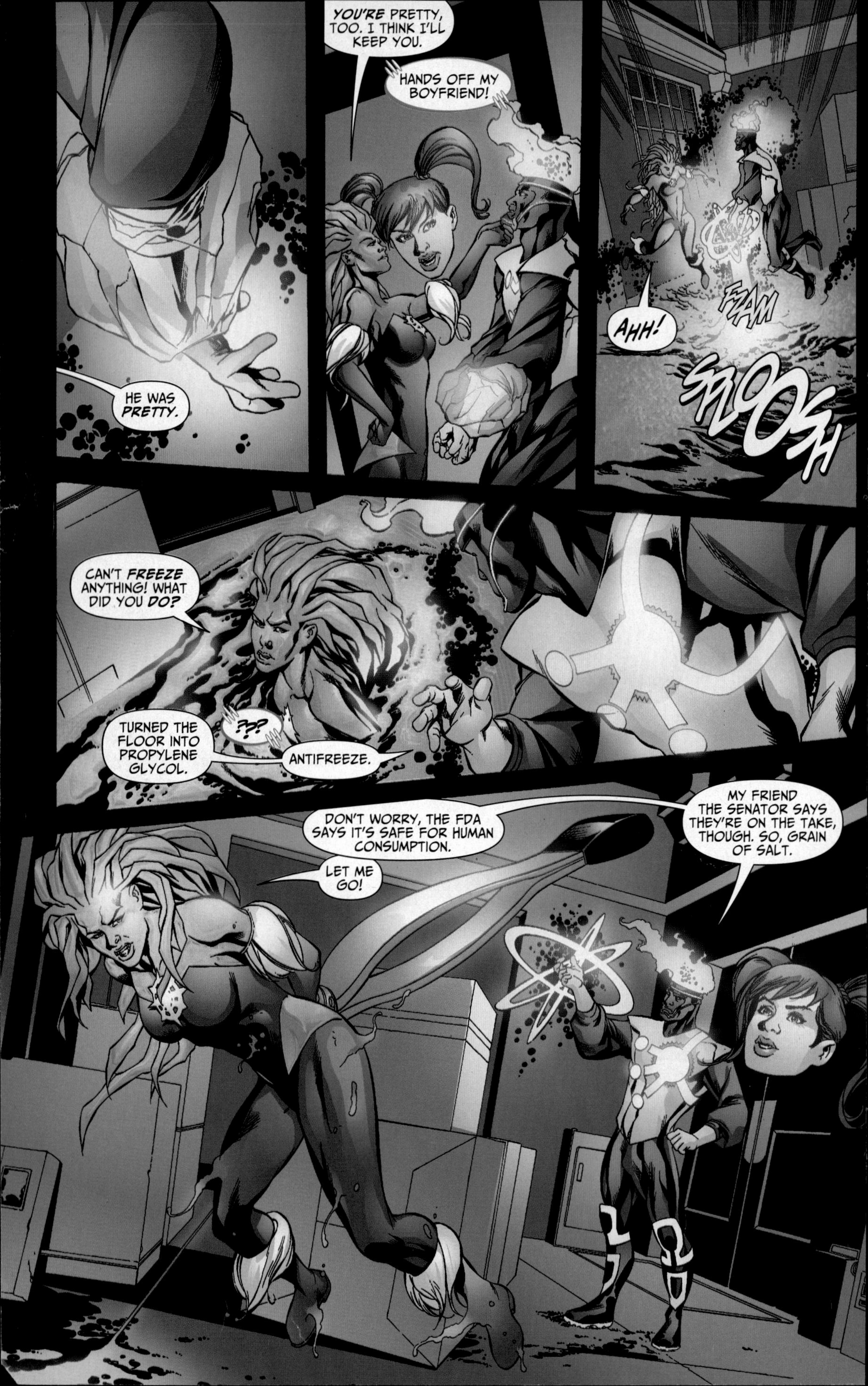
HE WAS PRETTY.
YOU'RE PRETTY, TOO. I THINK I'LL KEEP YOU.
HANDS OFF MY BOYFRIEND!
AHH!
FZAM
SPLOOOSH
CAN'T FREEZE ANYTHING! WHAT DID YOU DO?
TURNED THE FLOOR INTO PROPYLENE GLYCOL.
???
ANTIFREEZE.
DON'T WORRY, THE FDA SAYS IT'S SAFE FOR HUMAN CONSUMPTION.
MY FRIEND THE SENATOR SAYS THEY'RE ON THE TAKE, THOUGH. SO, GRAIN OF SALT.
LET ME GO!

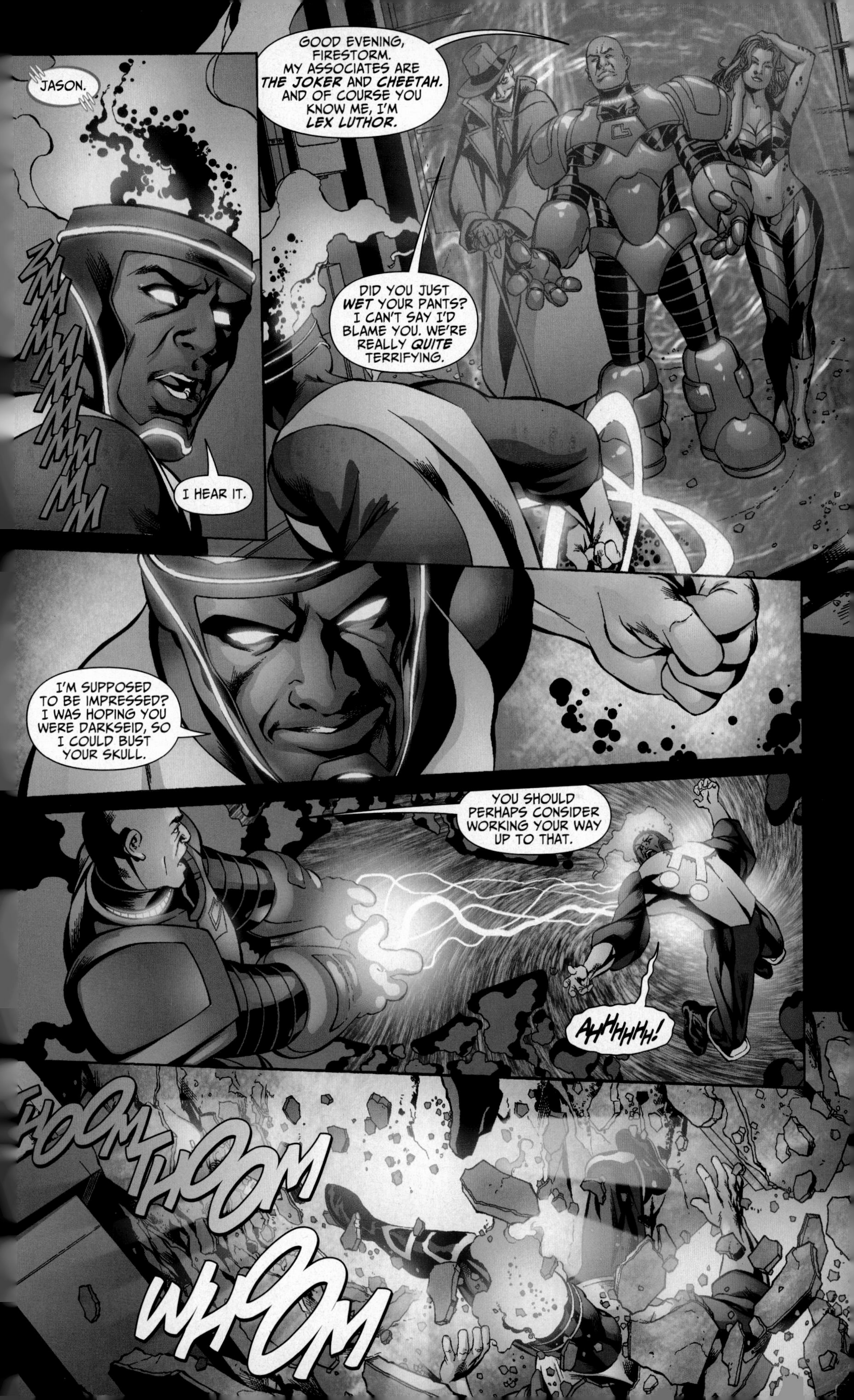
JASON.
GOOD EVENING, FIRESTORM. MY ASSOCIATES ARE THE JOKER AND CHEETAH. AND OF COURSE YOU KNOW ME, I'M LEX LUTHOR.
DID YOU JUST WET YOUR PANTS? I CAN'T SAY I'D BLAME YOU. WE'RE REALLY QUITE TERRIFYING.
I HEAR IT.
I'M SUPPOSED TO BE IMPRESSED? I WAS HOPING YOU WERE DARKSEID, SO I COULD BUST YOUR SKULL.
YOU SHOULD PERHAPS CONSIDER WORKING YOUR WAY UP TO THAT.
AHHHHHH!
WHOOM
WHOOM
WHOOM

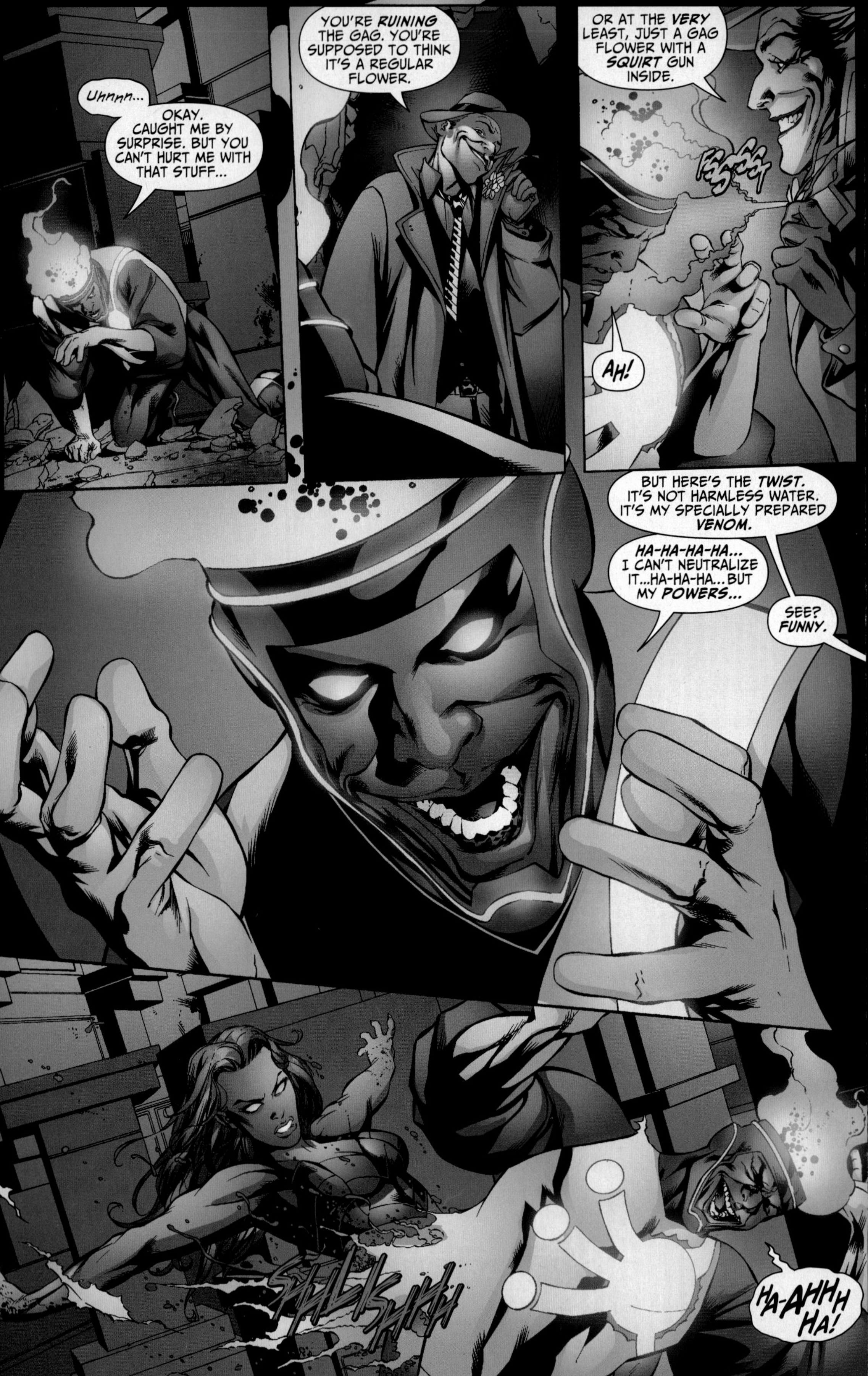
Uhnnn...
OKAY. CAUGHT ME BY SURPRISE. BUT YOU CAN'T HURT ME WITH THAT STUFF...
YOU'RE RUINING THE GAG. YOU'RE SUPPOSED TO THINK IT'S A REGULAR FLOWER.
OR AT THE VERY LEAST, JUST A GAG FLOWER WITH A SQUIRT GUN INSIDE.
FSSSSS
AH!
BUT HERE'S THE TWIST. IT'S NOT HARMLESS WATER. IT'S MY SPECIALLY PREPARED VENOM.
HA-HA-HA-HA... I CAN'T NEUTRALIZE IT...HA-HA-HA... BUT MY POWERS...
SEE? FUNNY.
SHLISHHH
HA-AHHH HA!

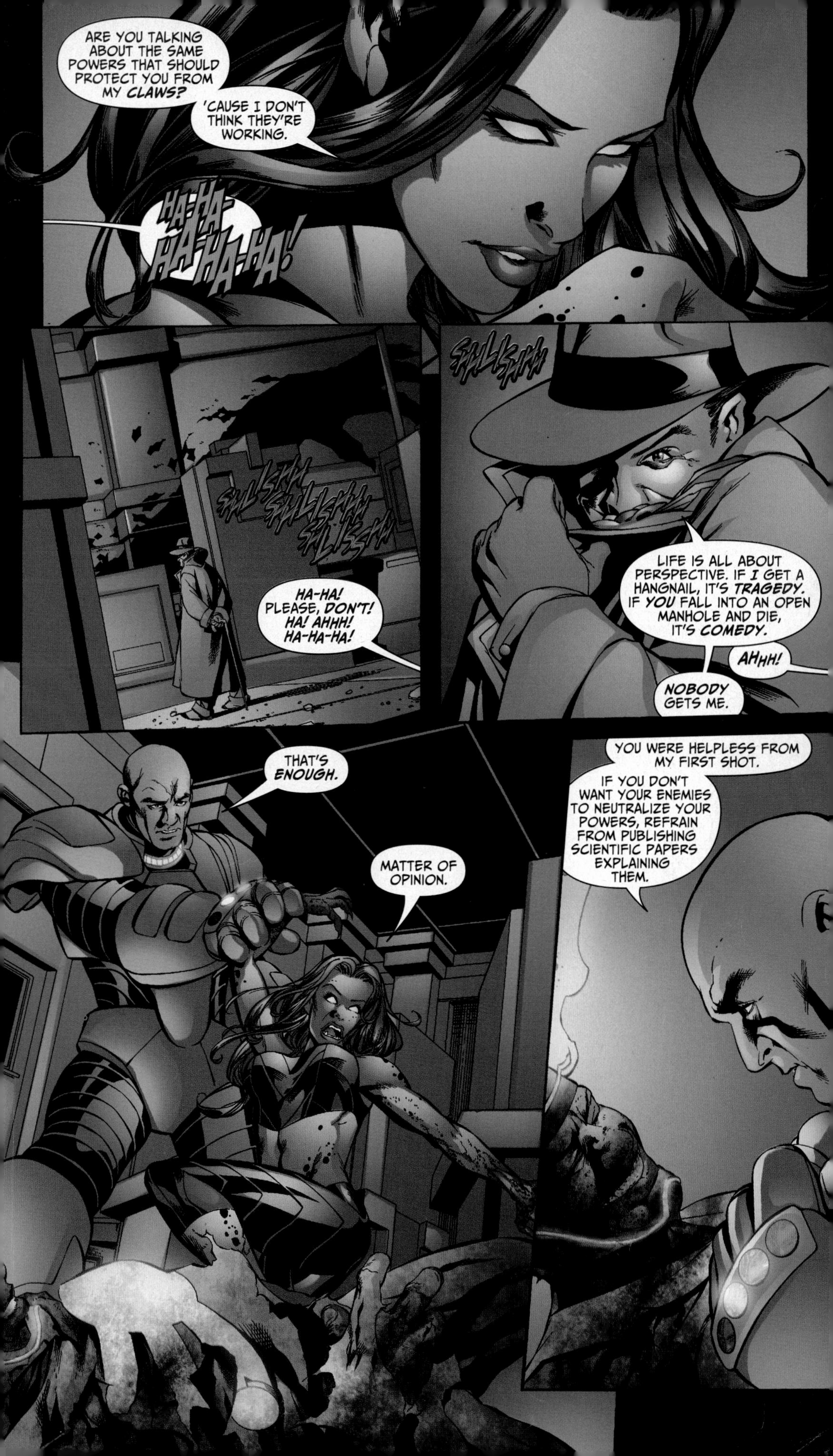

ARE YOU TALKING ABOUT THE SAME POWERS THAT SHOULD PROTECT YOU FROM MY *CLAWS?*
'CAUSE I DON'T THINK THEY'RE WORKING.
HA-HA-HA-HA-HA!
SHLISHH SHLISHH SHLISHH
HA-HA! PLEASE, *DON'T!* HA! AHHH! HA-HA-HA!
SHLISHH
LIFE IS ALL ABOUT PERSPECTIVE. IF *I* GET A HANGNAIL, IT'S *TRAGEDY.* IF *YOU* FALL INTO AN OPEN MANHOLE AND DIE, IT'S *COMEDY.*
AHHH!
NOBODY GETS ME.
THAT'S *ENOUGH.*
MATTER OF OPINION.
YOU WERE HELPLESS FROM MY FIRST SHOT.
IF YOU DON'T WANT YOUR ENEMIES TO NEUTRALIZE YOUR POWERS, REFRAIN FROM PUBLISHING SCIENTIFIC PAPERS EXPLAINING THEM.

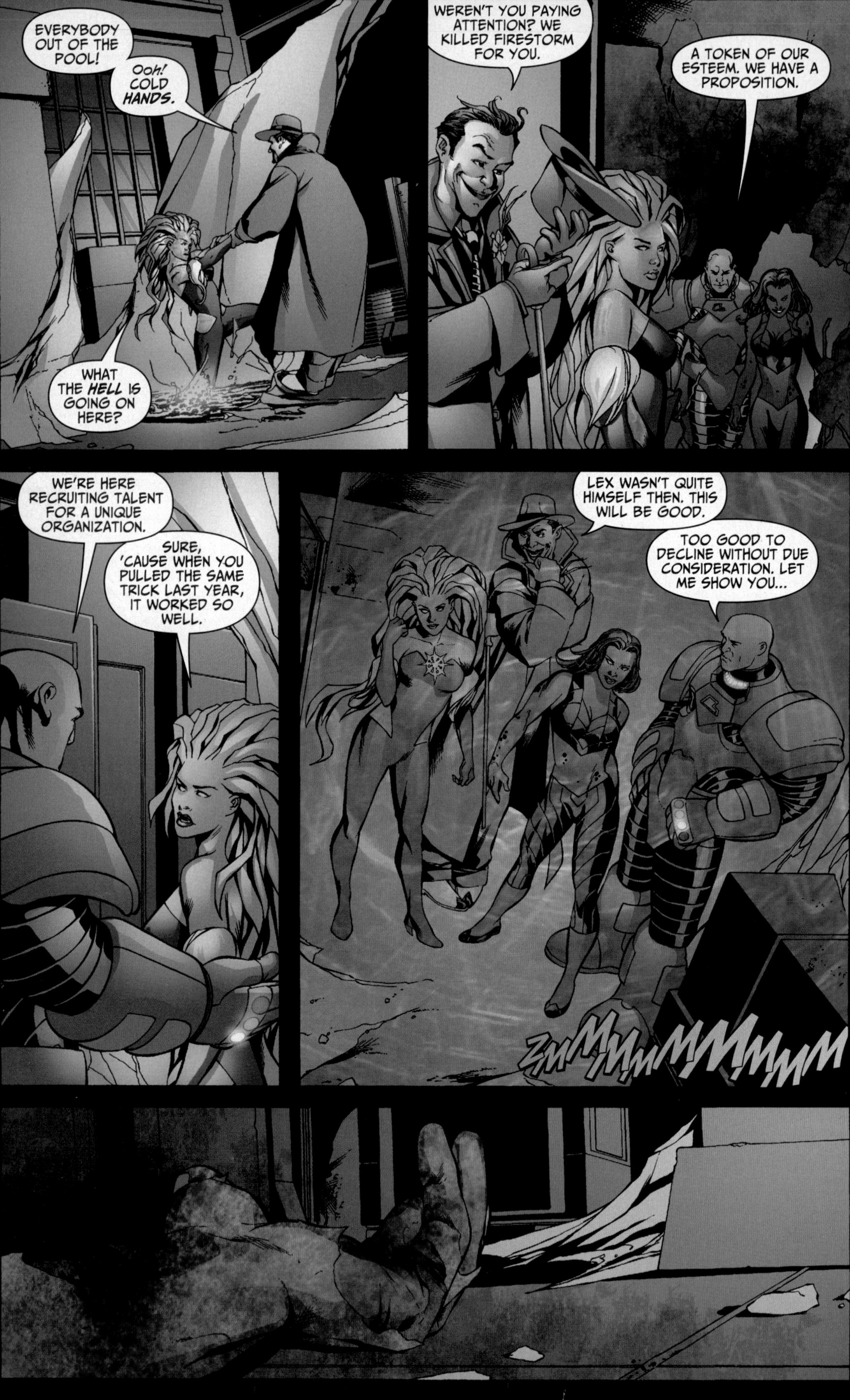
EVERYBODY OUT OF THE POOL!
Ooh! COLD HANDS.
WHAT THE HELL IS GOING ON HERE?
WEREN'T YOU PAYING ATTENTION? WE KILLED FIRESTORM FOR YOU.
A TOKEN OF OUR ESTEEM. WE HAVE A PROPOSITION.
WE'RE HERE RECRUITING TALENT FOR A UNIQUE ORGANIZATION.
SURE, 'CAUSE WHEN YOU PULLED THE SAME TRICK LAST YEAR, IT WORKED SO WELL.
LEX WASN'T QUITE HIMSELF THEN. THIS WILL BE GOOD.
TOO GOOD TO DECLINE WITHOUT DUE CONSIDERATION. LET ME SHOW YOU...
ZMMMMMMMMMMMMMM

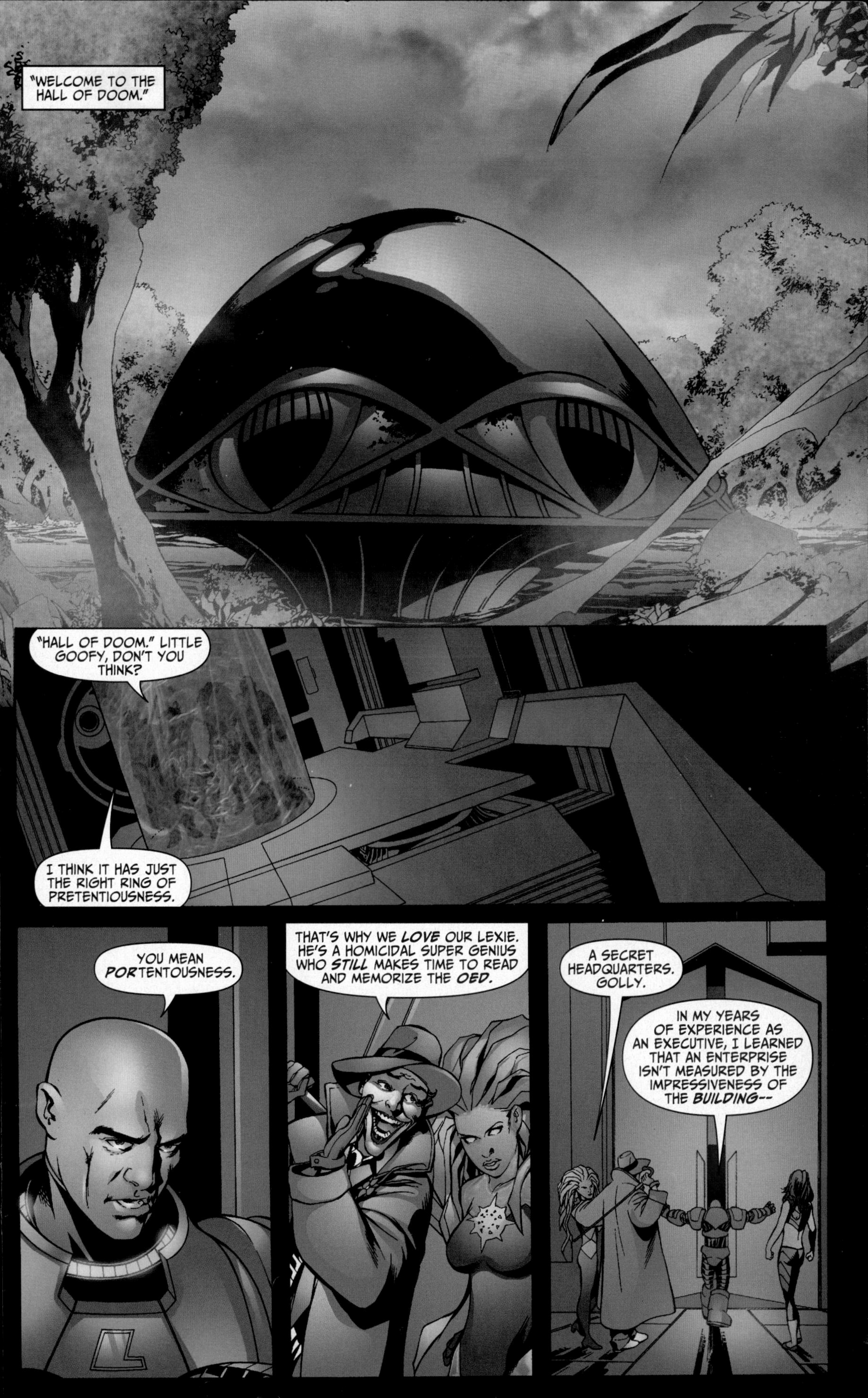

"WELCOME TO THE HALL OF DOOM."
"HALL OF DOOM." LITTLE GOOFY, DON'T YOU THINK?
I THINK IT HAS JUST THE RIGHT RING OF PRETENTIOUSNESS.
YOU MEAN *POR*TENTOUSNESS.
THAT'S WHY WE *LOVE* OUR LEXIE. HE'S A HOMICIDAL SUPER GENIUS WHO *STILL* MAKES TIME TO READ AND MEMORIZE THE *OED.*
A SECRET HEADQUARTERS. GOLLY.
IN MY YEARS OF EXPERIENCE AS AN EXECUTIVE, I LEARNED THAT AN ENTERPRISE ISN'T MEASURED BY THE IMPRESSIVENESS OF THE *BUILDING--*

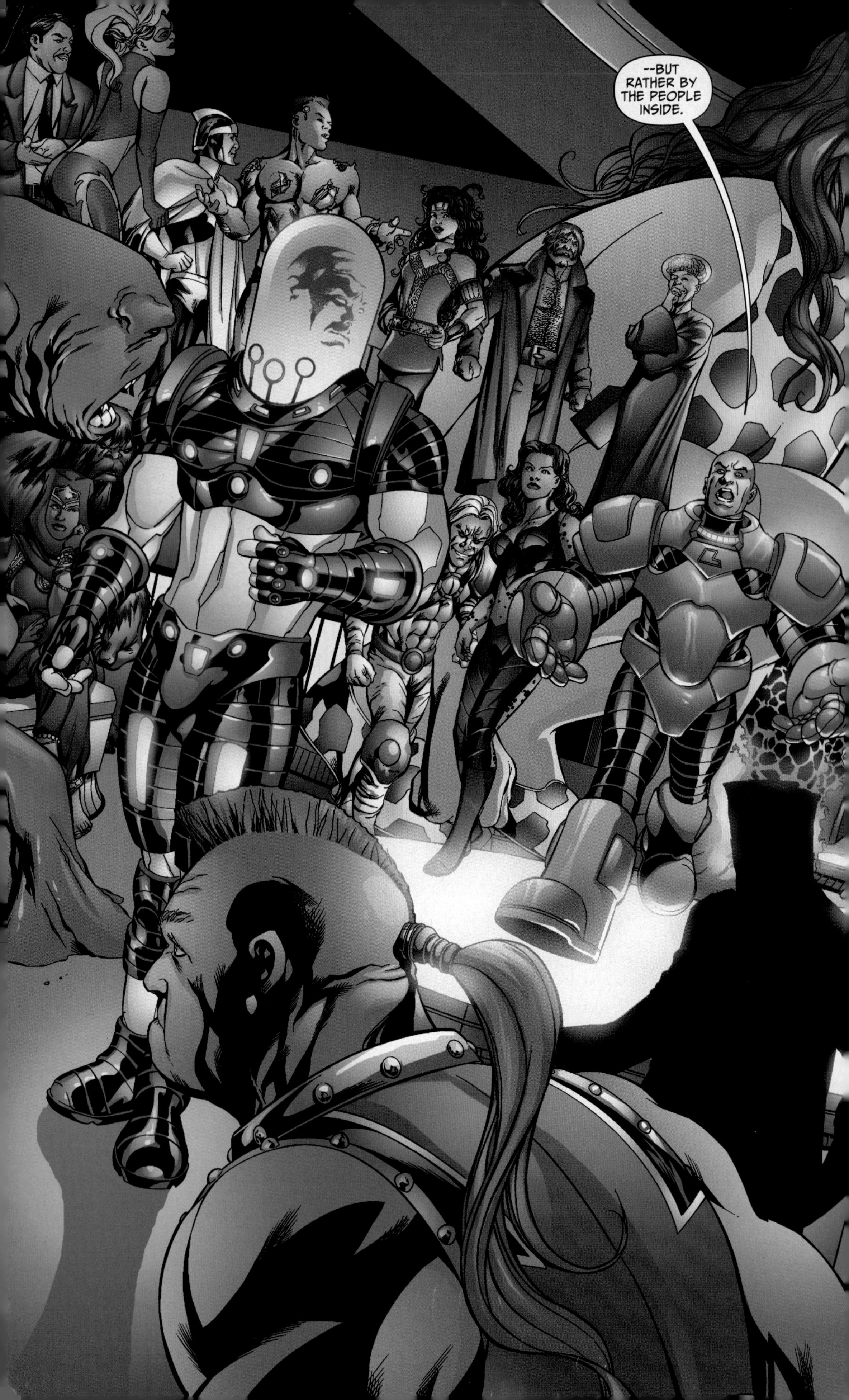
--BUT RATHER BY THE PEOPLE INSIDE.

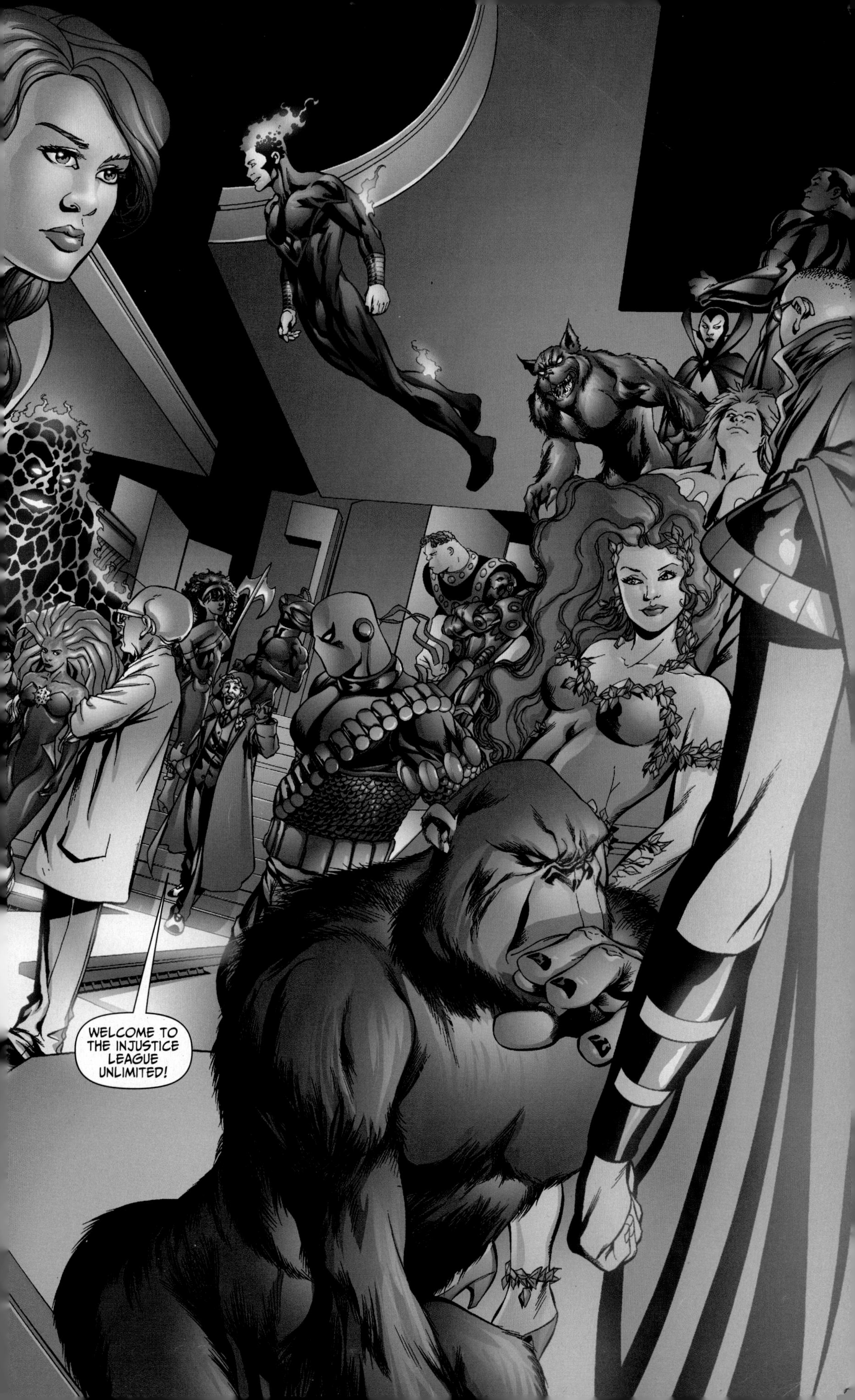
WELCOME TO THE INJUSTICE LEAGUE UNLIMITED!

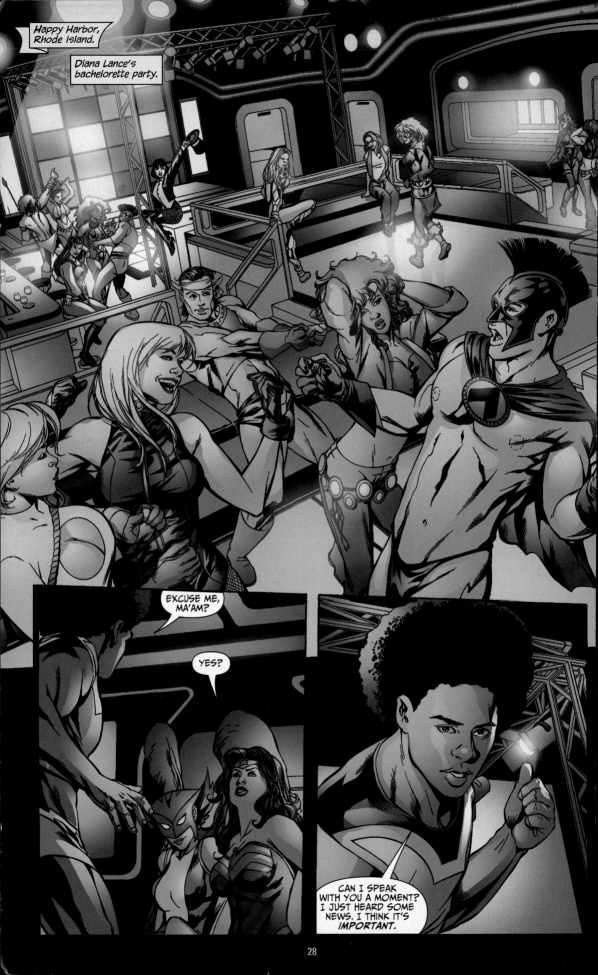

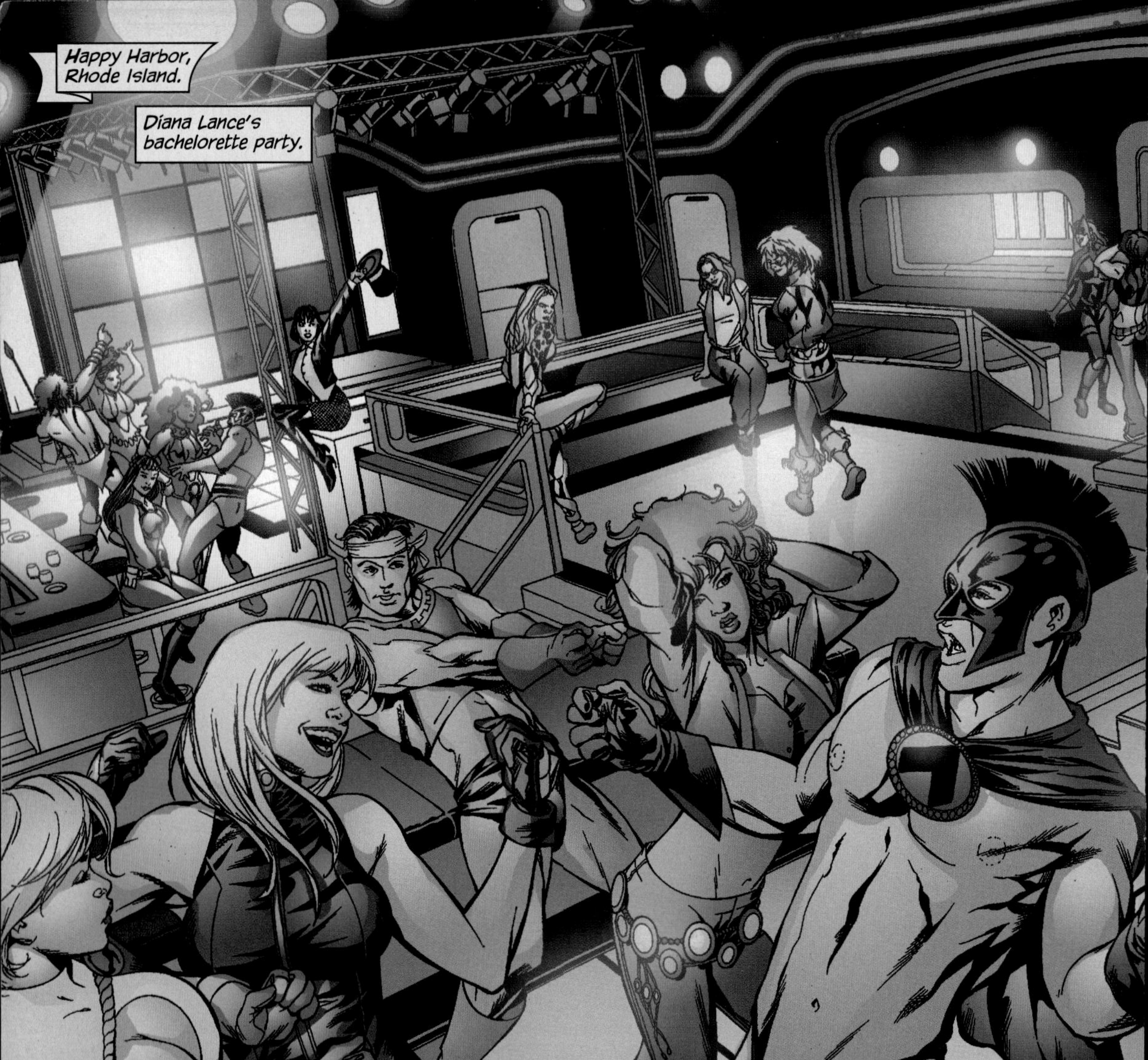
Happy Harbor, Rhode Island.
Diana Lance's bachelorette party.
EXCUSE ME, MA'AM?
YES?
CAN I SPEAK WITH YOU A MOMENT? I JUST HEARD SOME NEWS. I THINK IT'S *IMPORTANT*.

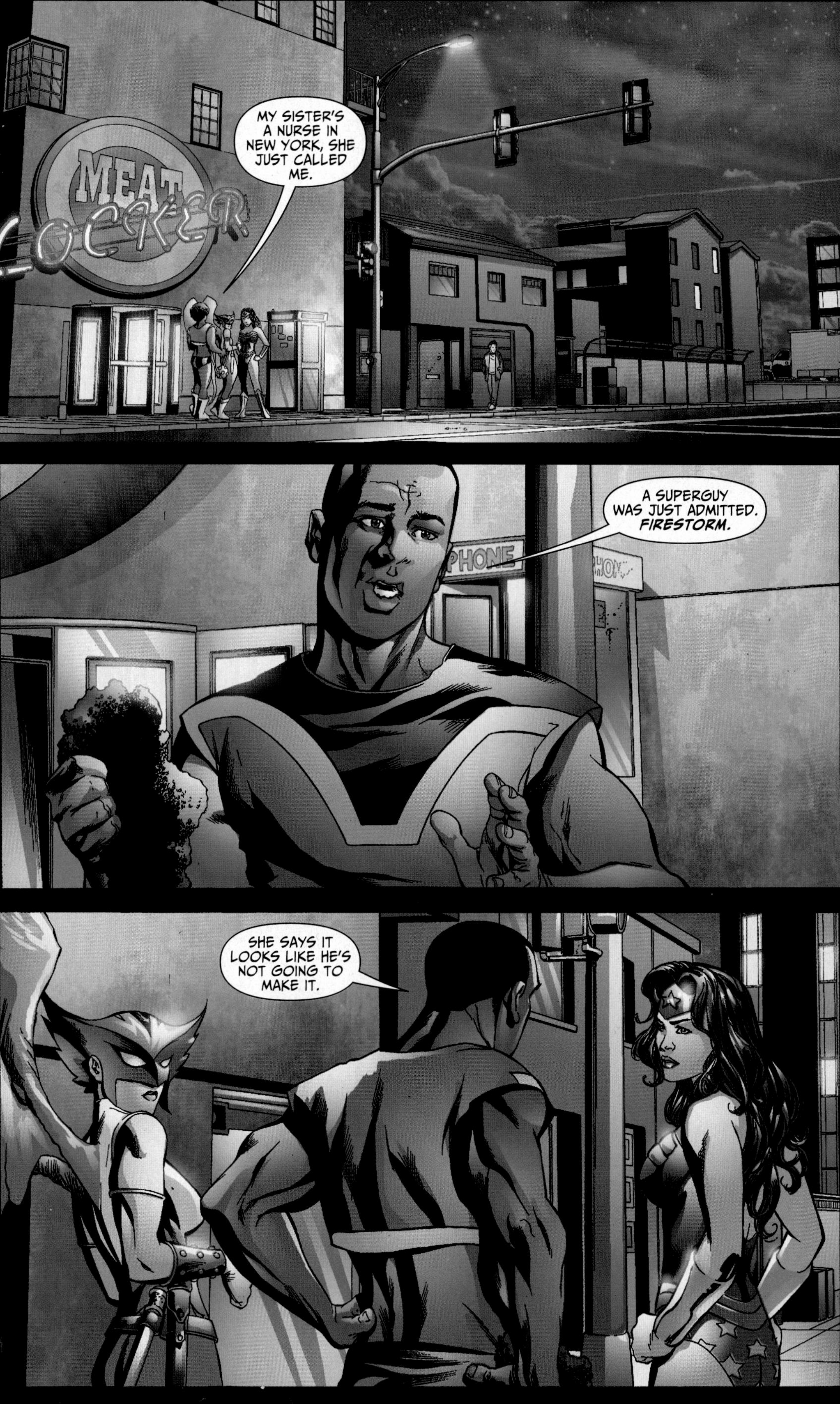
MEAT
LOCKER
MY SISTER'S A NURSE IN NEW YORK, SHE JUST CALLED ME.
PHONE
A SUPERGUY WAS JUST ADMITTED. *FIRESTORM.*
SHE SAYS IT LOOKS LIKE HE'S NOT GOING TO MAKE IT.

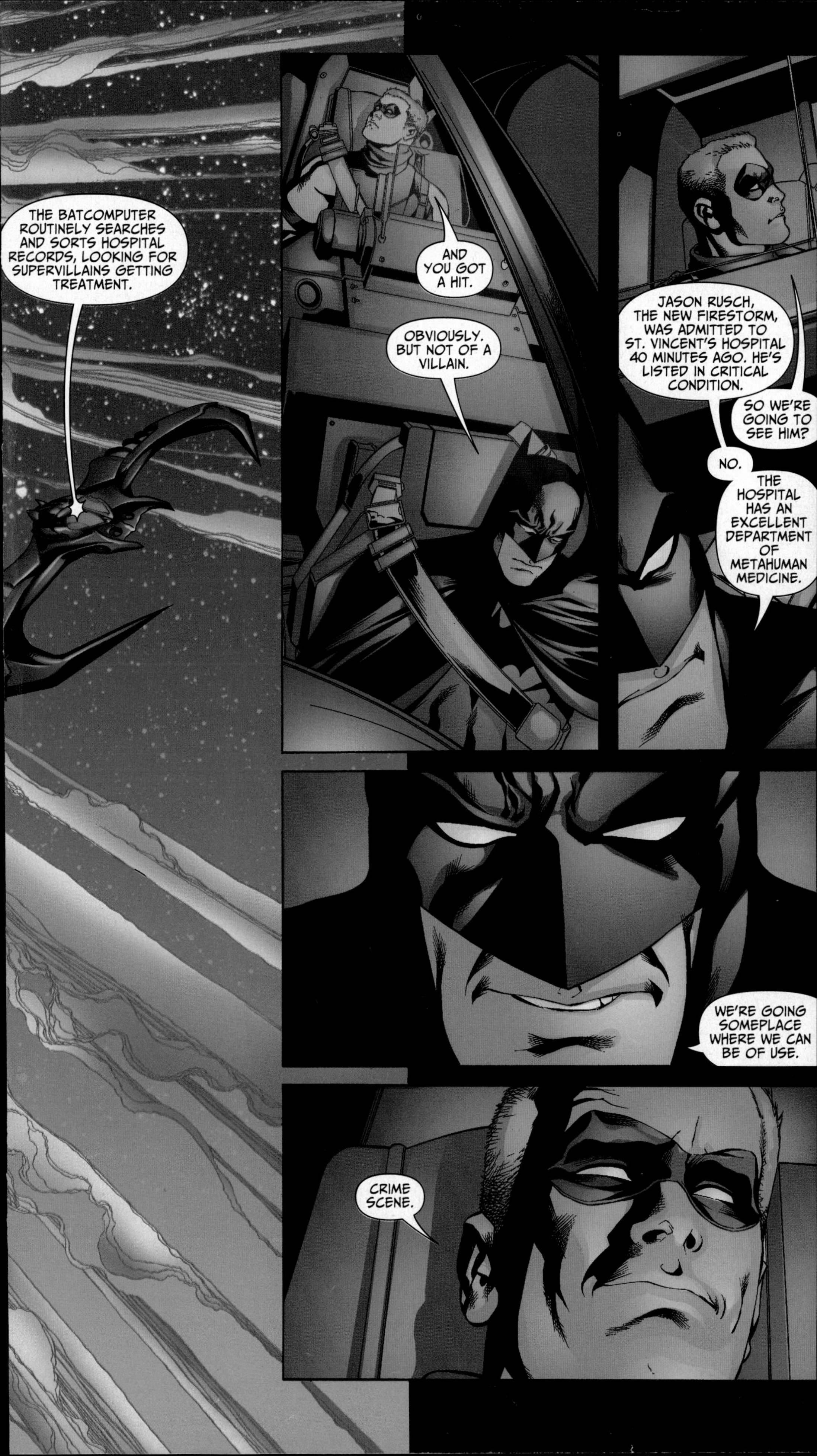
THE BATCOMPUTER ROUTINELY SEARCHES AND SORTS HOSPITAL RECORDS, LOOKING FOR SUPERVILLAINS GETTING TREATMENT.
AND YOU GOT A HIT.
OBVIOUSLY. BUT NOT OF A VILLAIN.
JASON RUSCH, THE NEW FIRESTORM, WAS ADMITTED TO ST. VINCENT'S HOSPITAL 40 MINUTES AGO. HE'S LISTED IN CRITICAL CONDITION.
SO WE'RE GOING TO SEE HIM?
NO.
THE HOSPITAL HAS AN EXCELLENT DEPARTMENT OF METAHUMAN MEDICINE.
WE'RE GOING SOMEPLACE WHERE WE CAN BE OF USE.
CRIME SCENE.

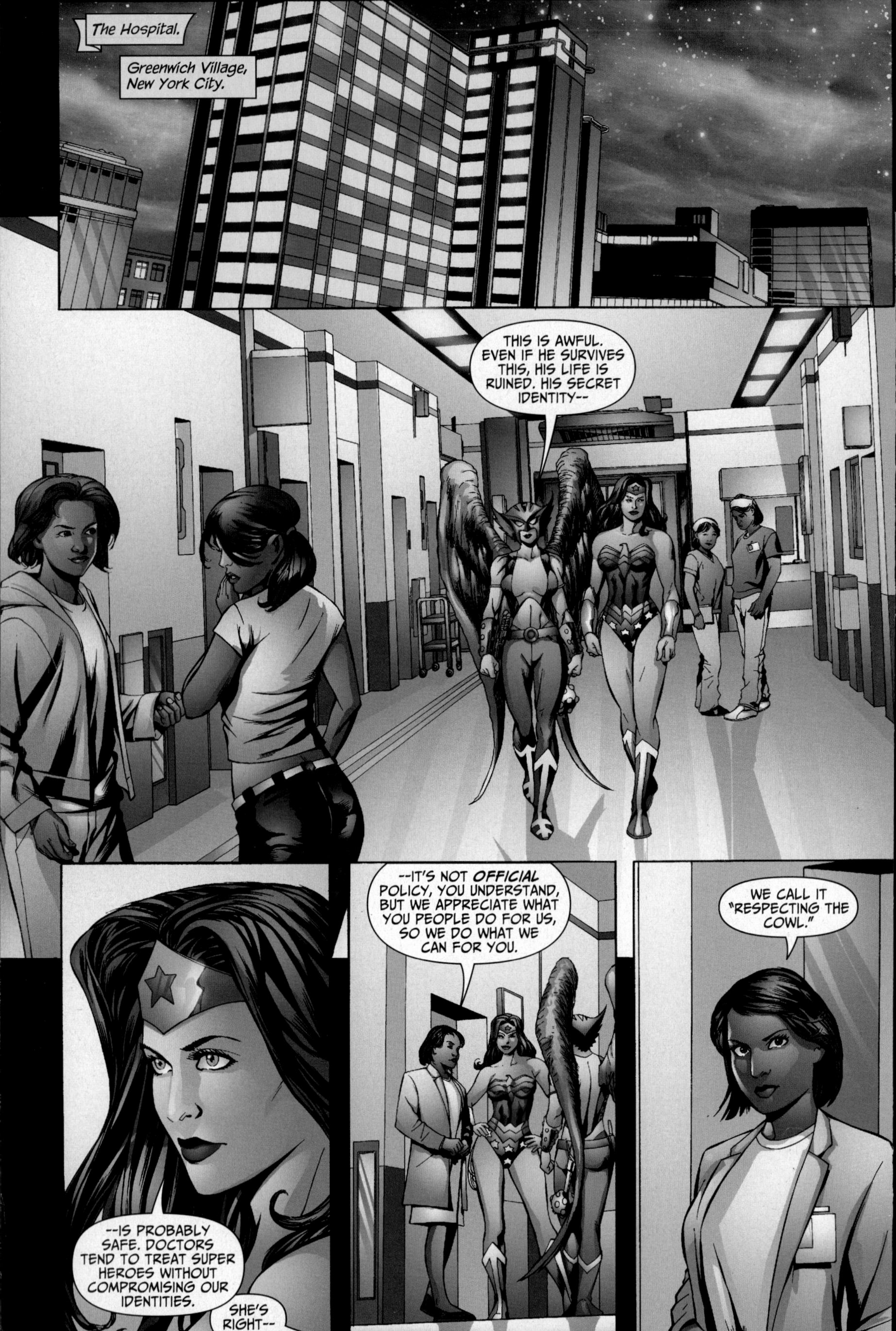
The Hospital.
Greenwich Village, New York City.
THIS IS AWFUL. EVEN IF HE SURVIVES THIS, HIS LIFE IS RUINED. HIS SECRET IDENTITY--
--IS PROBABLY SAFE. DOCTORS TEND TO TREAT SUPER HEROES WITHOUT COMPROMISING OUR IDENTITIES.
SHE'S RIGHT--
--IT'S NOT *OFFICIAL* POLICY, YOU UNDERSTAND, BUT WE APPRECIATE WHAT YOU PEOPLE DO FOR US, SO WE DO WHAT WE CAN FOR YOU.
WE CALL IT "RESPECTING THE COWL."

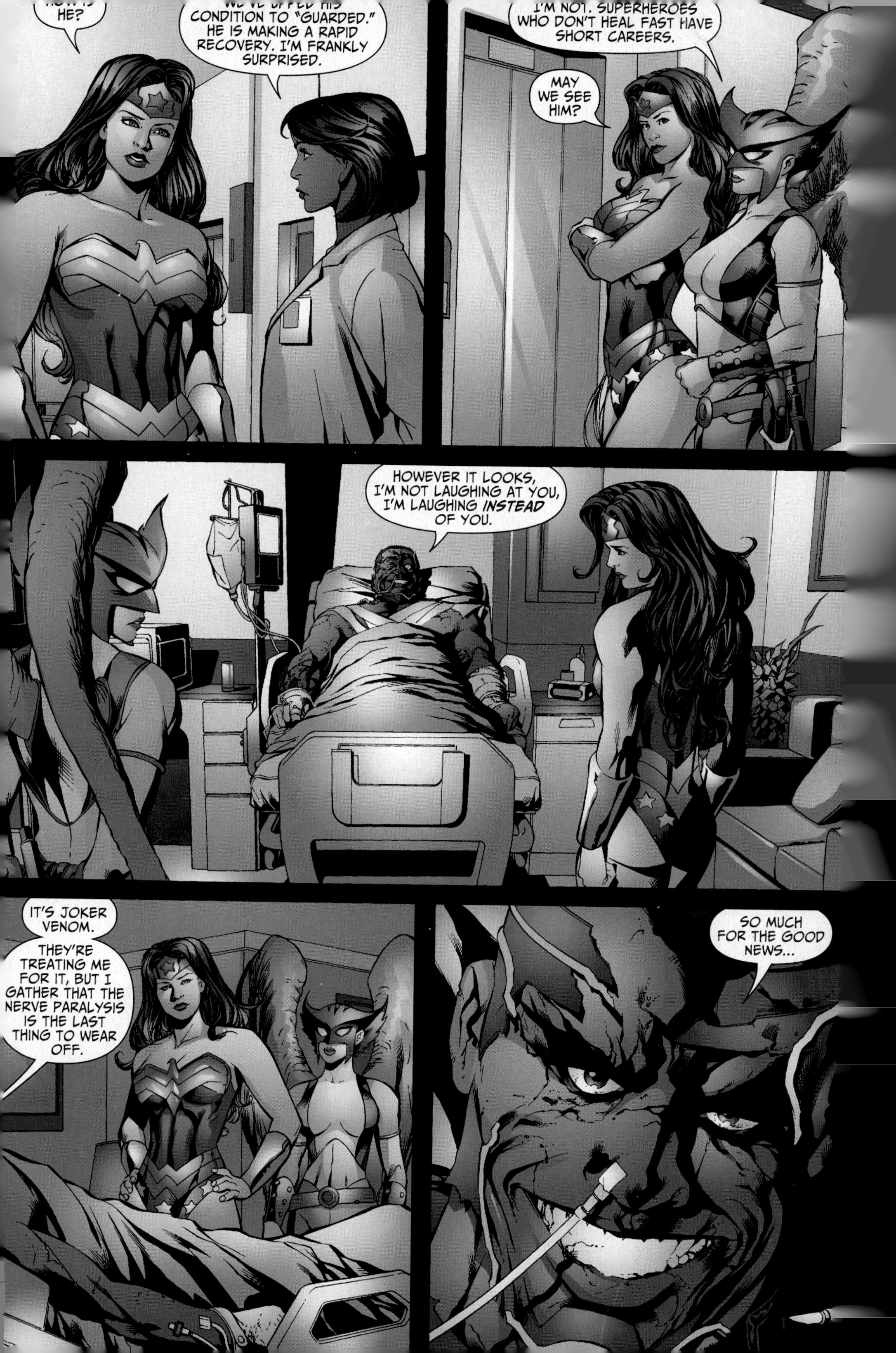
HE?
CONDITION TO "GUARDED." HE IS MAKING A RAPID RECOVERY. I'M FRANKLY SURPRISED.
I'M NOT. SUPERHEROES WHO DON'T HEAL FAST HAVE SHORT CAREERS.
MAY WE SEE HIM?
HOWEVER IT LOOKS, I'M NOT LAUGHING AT YOU, I'M LAUGHING *INSTEAD* OF YOU.
IT'S JOKER VENOM.
THEY'RE TREATING ME FOR IT, BUT I GATHER THAT THE NERVE PARALYSIS IS THE LAST THING TO WEAR OFF.
SO MUCH FOR THE GOOD NEWS...

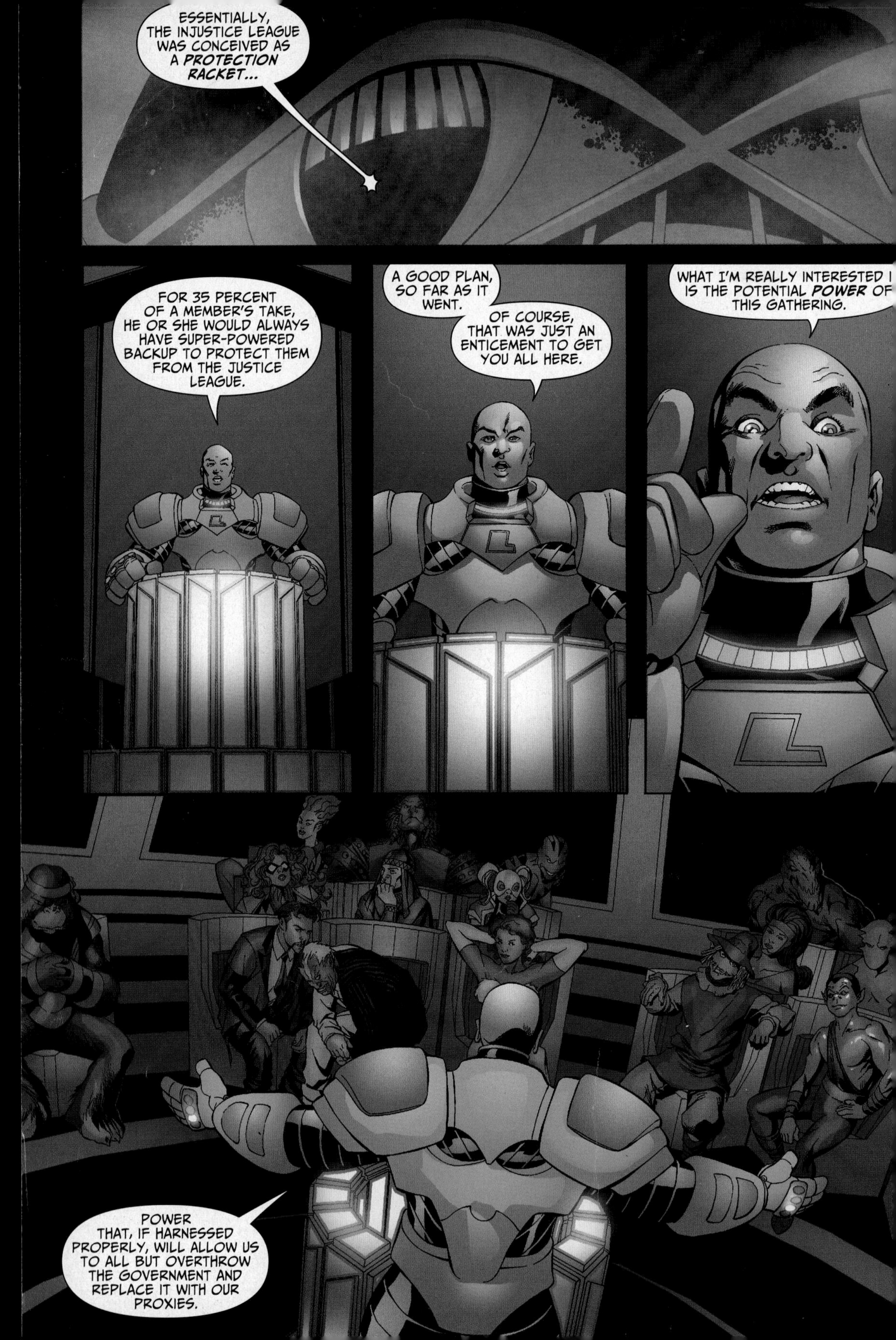
ESSENTIALLY, THE INJUSTICE LEAGUE WAS CONCEIVED AS A PROTECTION RACKET...
FOR 35 PERCENT OF A MEMBER'S TAKE, HE OR SHE WOULD ALWAYS HAVE SUPER-POWERED BACKUP TO PROTECT THEM FROM THE JUSTICE LEAGUE.
A GOOD PLAN, SO FAR AS IT WENT.
OF COURSE, THAT WAS JUST AN ENTICEMENT TO GET YOU ALL HERE.
WHAT I'M REALLY INTERESTED I IS THE POTENTIAL POWER OF THIS GATHERING.
POWER THAT, IF HARNESSED PROPERLY, WILL ALLOW US TO ALL BUT OVERTHROW THE GOVERNMENT AND REPLACE IT WITH OUR PROXIES.

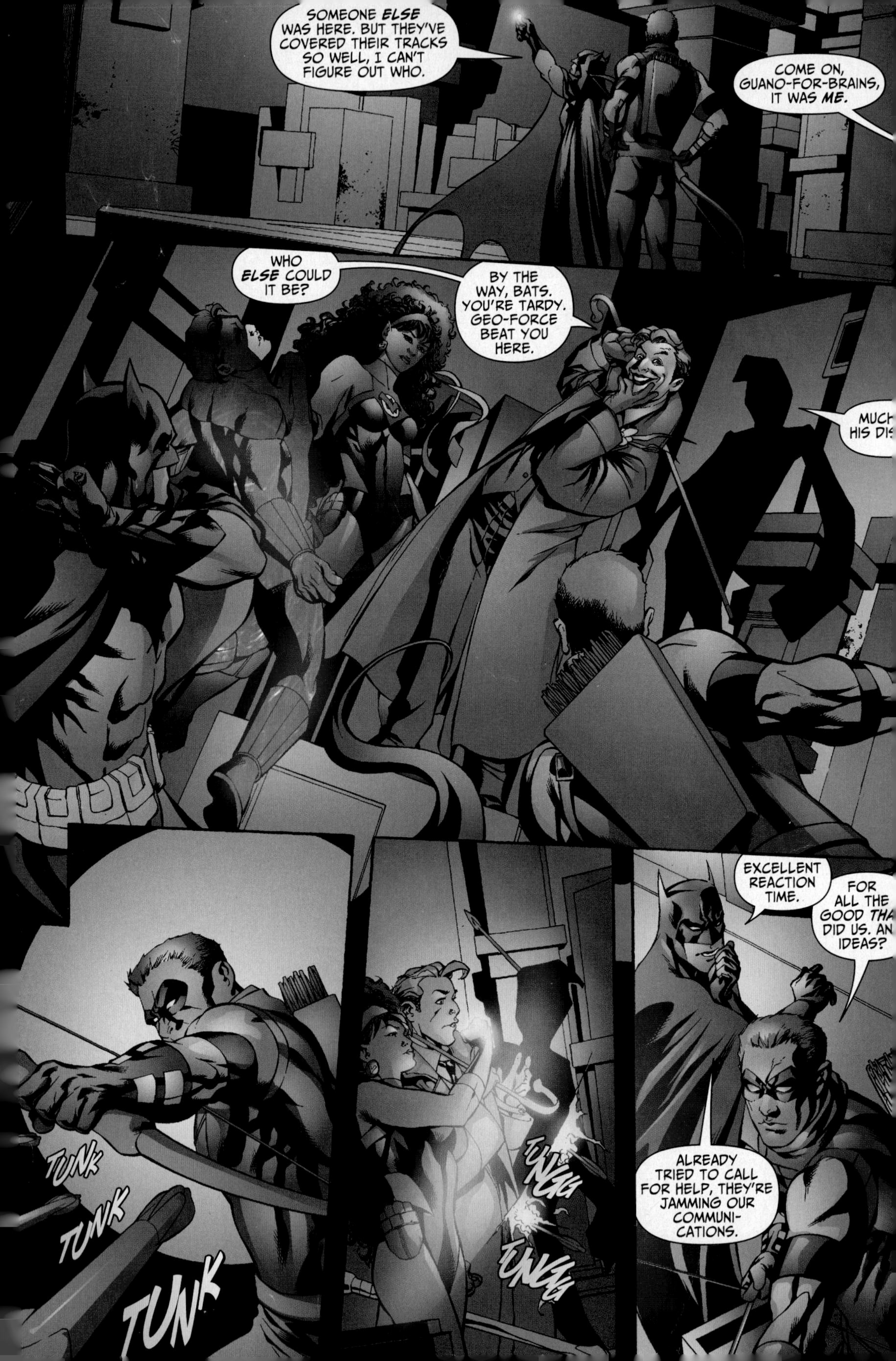

SOMEONE ELSE WAS HERE. BUT THEY'VE COVERED THEIR TRACKS SO WELL, I CAN'T FIGURE OUT WHO.
COME ON, GUANO-FOR-BRAINS, IT WAS ME.
WHO ELSE COULD IT BE?
BY THE WAY, BATS. YOU'RE TARDY. GEO-FORCE BEAT YOU HERE.
TUNK
TUNK
TUNK
TUNGG
TUNGG
EXCELLENT REACTION TIME.
ALREADY TRIED TO CALL FOR HELP, THEY'RE JAMMING OUR COMMUNI-CATIONS.

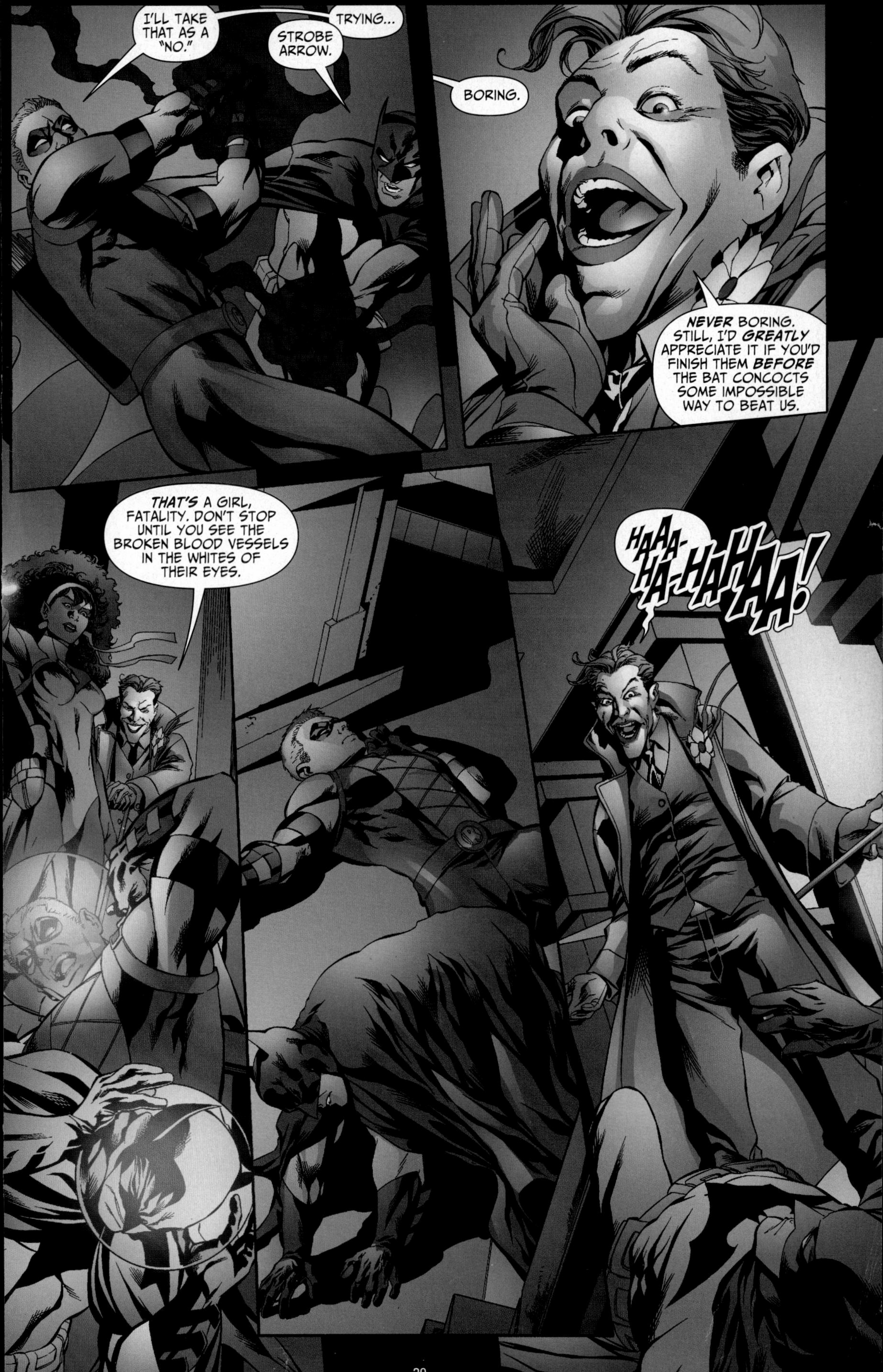
I'LL TAKE THAT AS A "NO."
TRYING...
STROBE ARROW.
BORING.
NEVER BORING. STILL, I'D GREATLY APPRECIATE IT IF YOU'D FINISH THEM BEFORE THE BAT CONCOCTS SOME IMPOSSIBLE WAY TO BEAT US.
THAT'S A GIRL, FATALITY. DON'T STOP UNTIL YOU SEE THE BROKEN BLOOD VESSELS IN THE WHITES OF THEIR EYES.
HAAAA-HA-HAHAHAA!

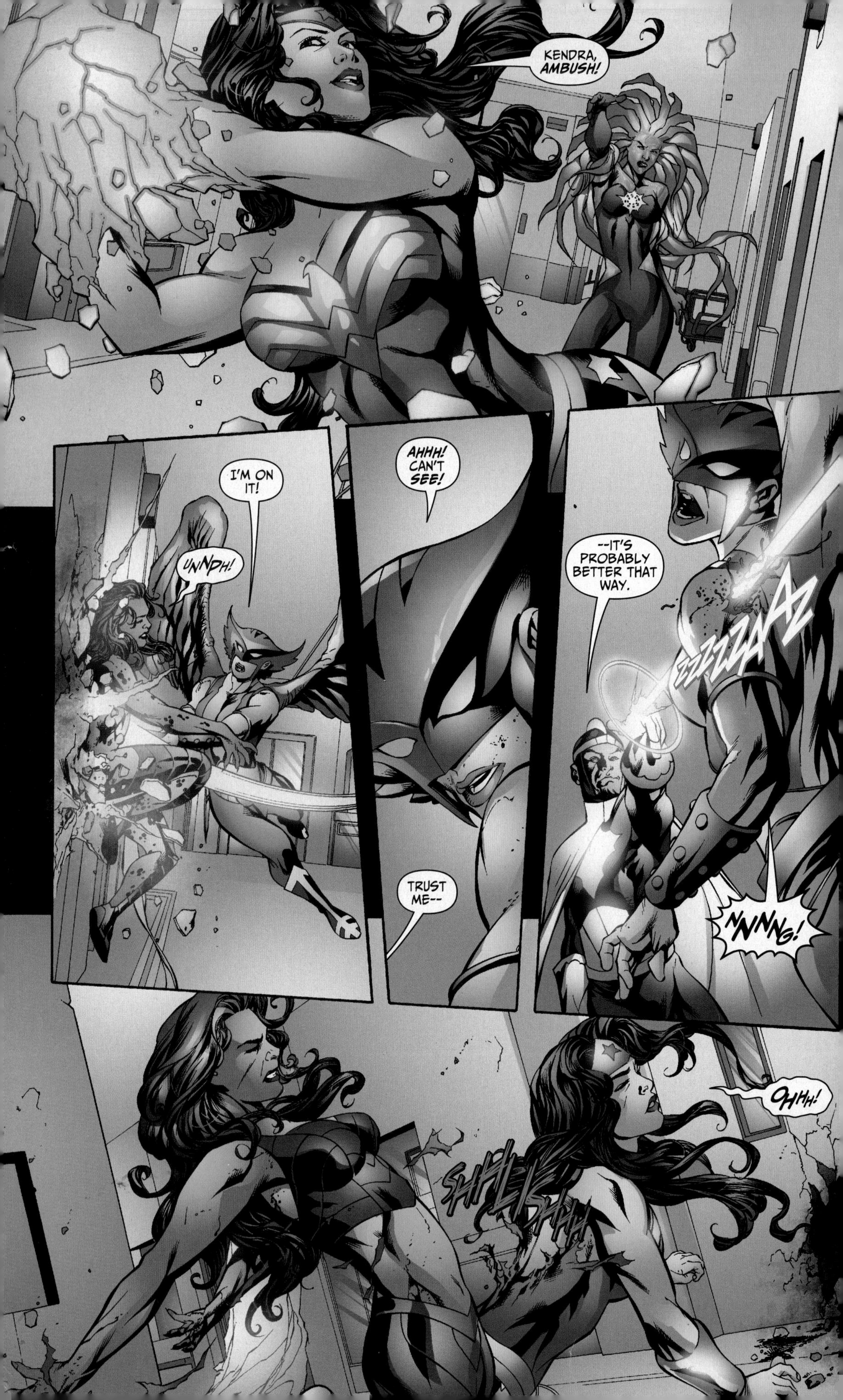
KENDRA, AMBUSH!
I'M ON IT!
UNNPH!
AHHH! CAN'T SEE!
TRUST ME--
--IT'S PROBABLY BETTER THAT WAY.
ZZZZZAAZ
NNNNG!
OHHH!
SHHLISHHH

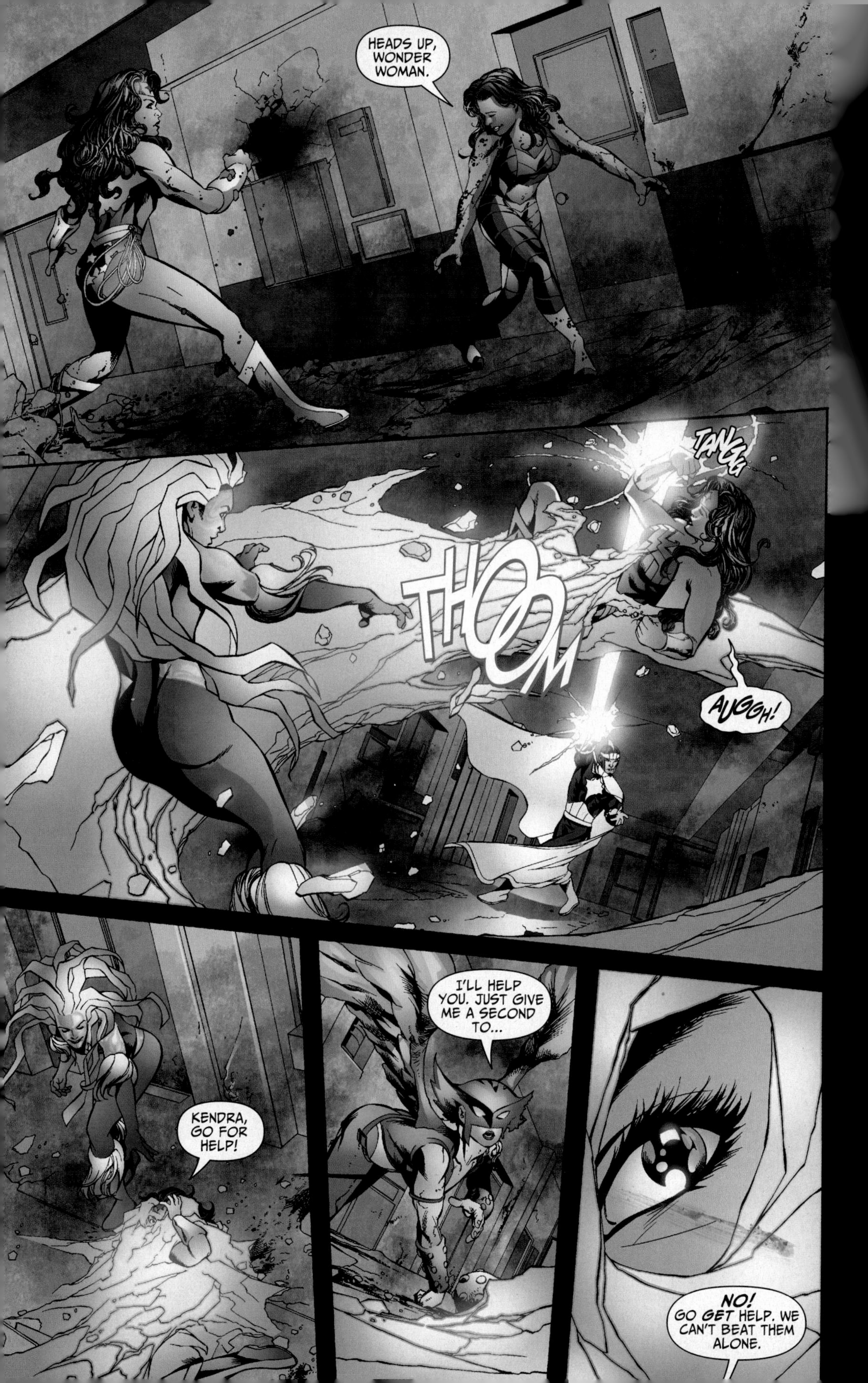
HEADS UP, WONDER WOMAN.
TANGG
THOOOM
AUGGH!
KENDRA, GO FOR HELP!
I'LL HELP YOU. JUST GIVE ME A SECOND TO...
NO! GO GET HELP. WE CAN'T BEAT THEM ALONE.

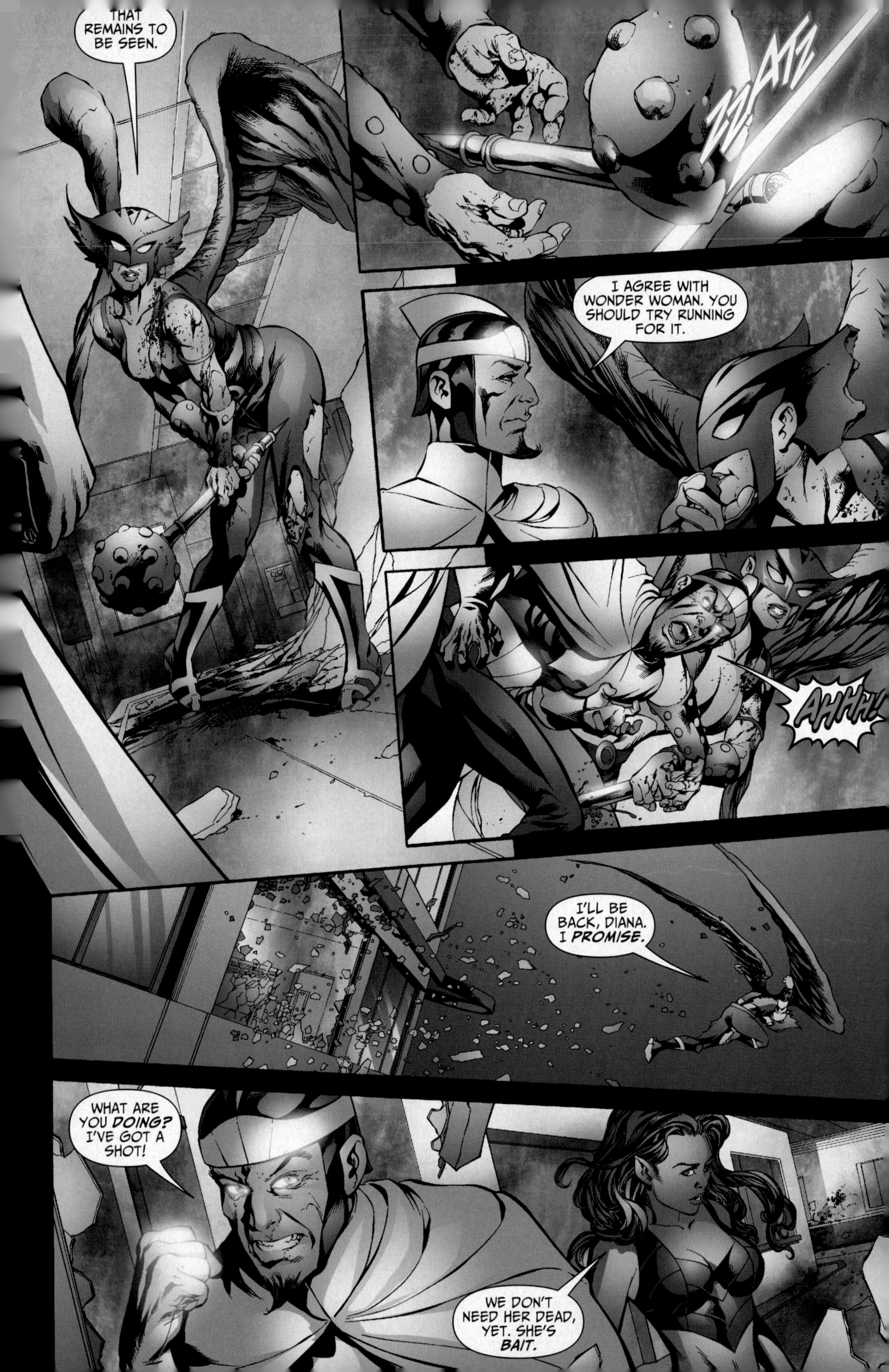
THAT REMAINS TO BE SEEN.
ZZAATZ
I AGREE WITH WONDER WOMAN. YOU SHOULD TRY RUNNING FOR IT.
AHHH!
I'LL BE BACK, DIANA. I *PROMISE*.
WHAT ARE YOU *DOING?* I'VE GOT A SHOT!
WE DON'T NEED HER DEAD, YET. SHE'S *BAIT*.

Hours later.

The Hall of Justice.

KISSSSSSH

WHAT HAPPENED?

ATTACKED. WONDER WOMAN'S IN TROUBLE... COULDN'T CALL FOR HELP. SOME KIND OF JAMMING...

CHEETAH AND DR. LIGHT...

...JOKER AND LUTHOR, THEY'RE ALL...

...WORKING TOGETHER...

IT'S OKAY. REST. WE GOT THIS.

YOU ALL HEARD THE MAN--

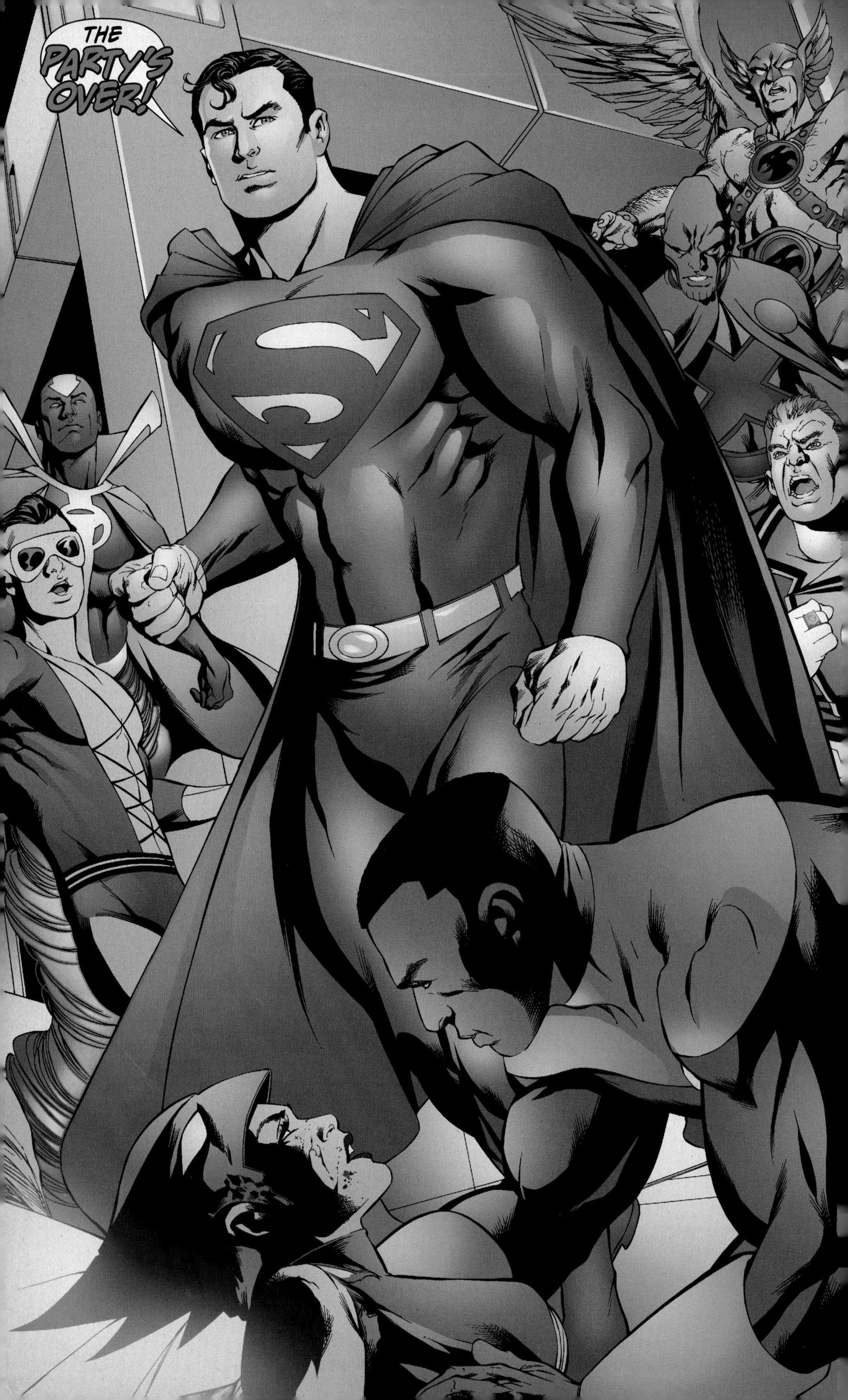
THE PARTY'S OVER!

JUSTICE LEAGUE of AMERICA

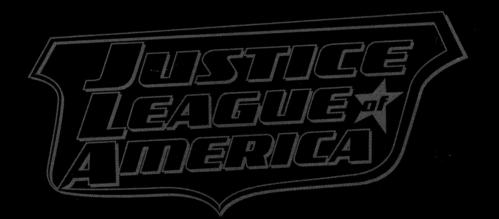

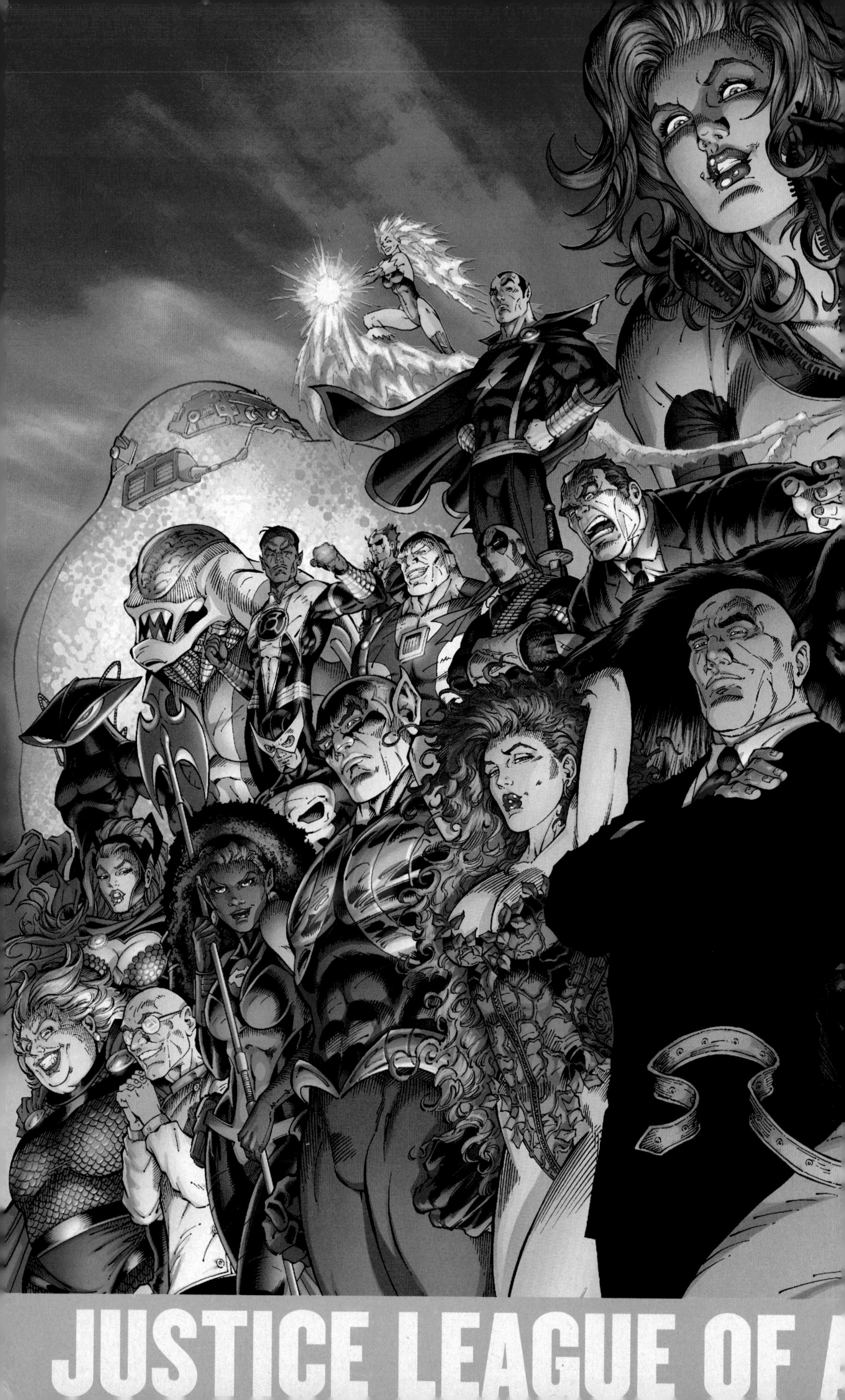
JUSTICE LEAGUE OF A

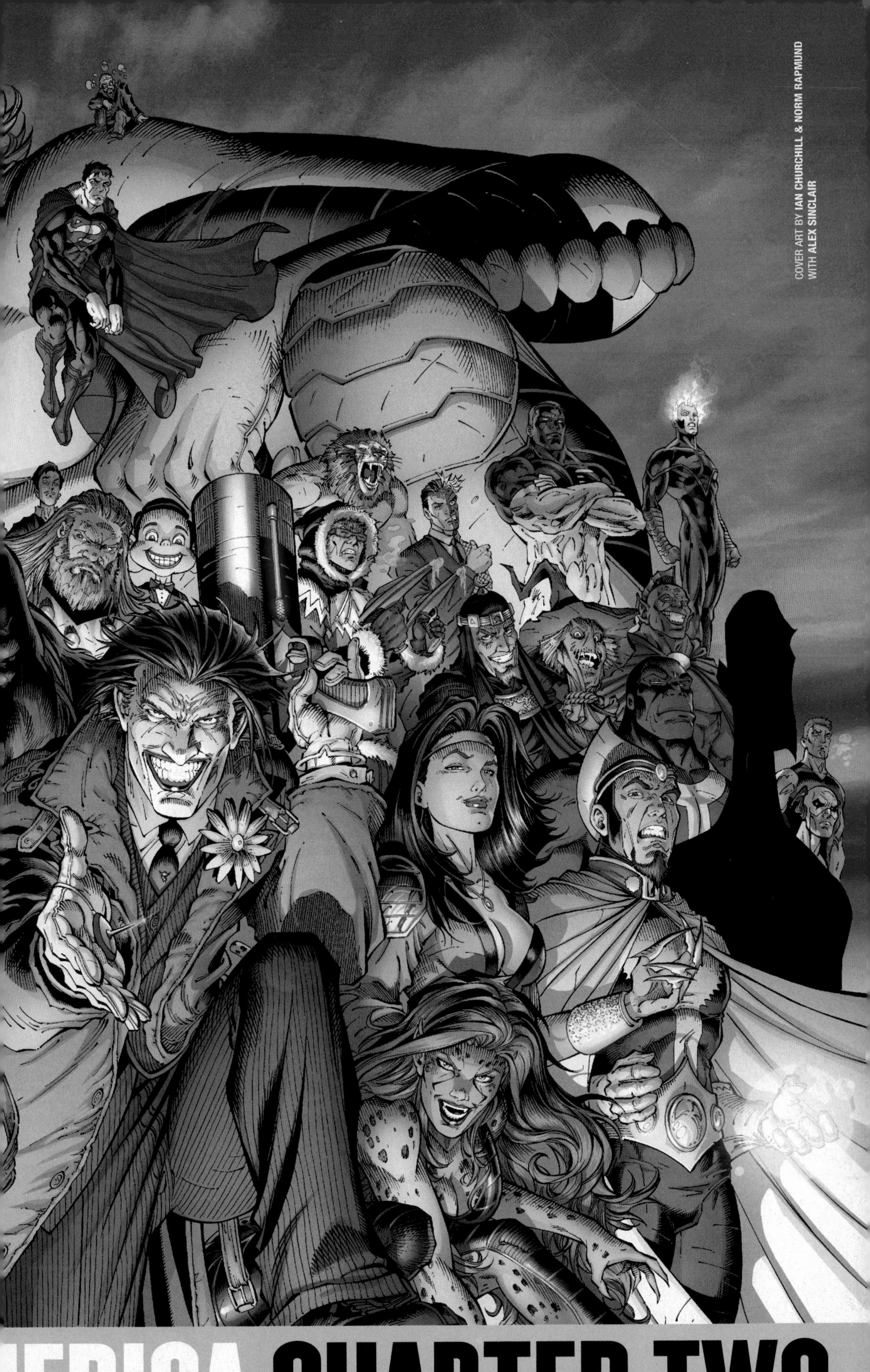
COVER ART BY IAN CHURCHILL & NORM RAPMUND
WITH ALEX SINCLAIR

ERICA CHAPTER TWO

"I don't know how to thank you. I—"

"Start by being honest with your teammates."

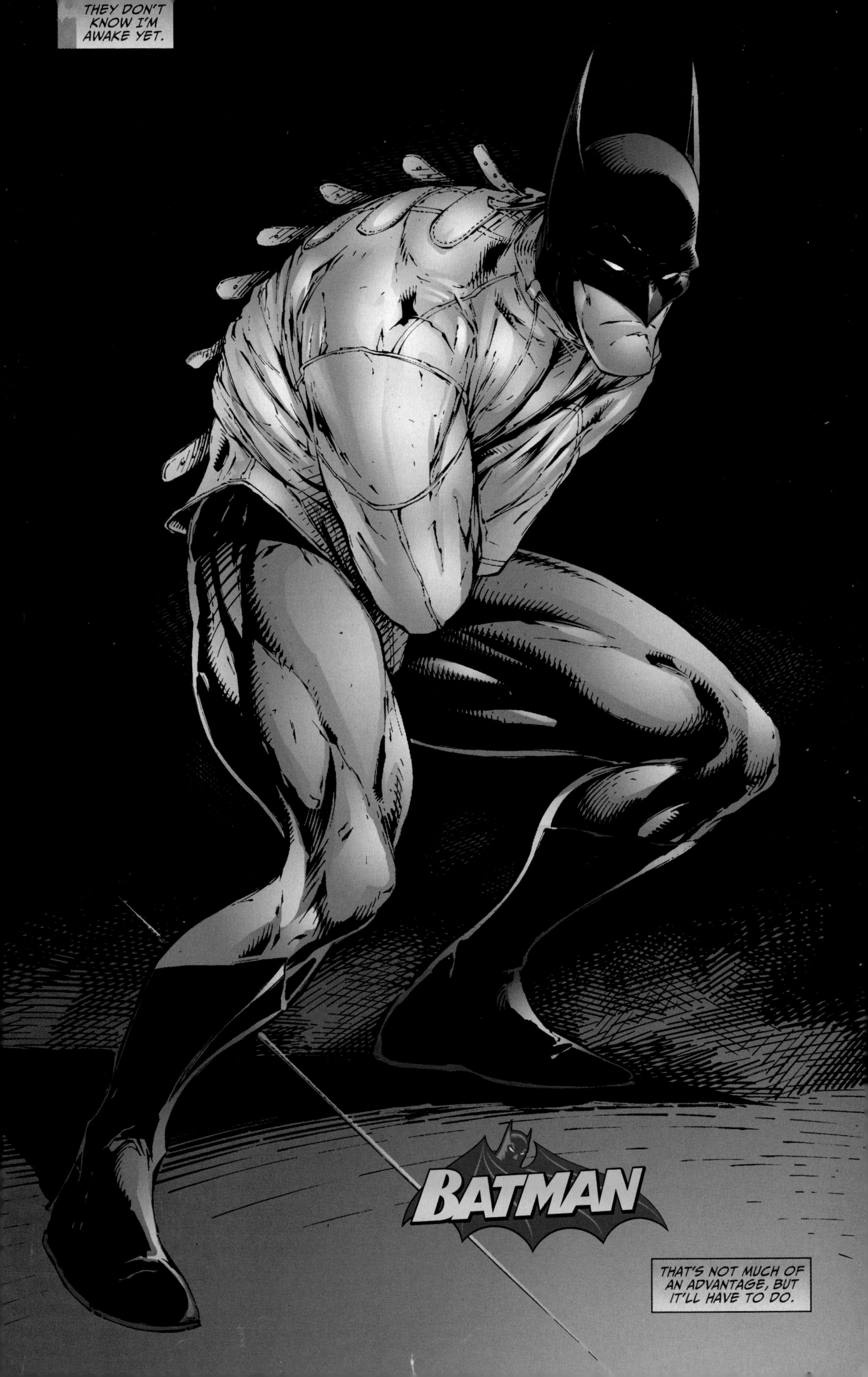
THEY DON'T KNOW I'M AWAKE YET.
BATMAN
THAT'S NOT MUCH OF AN ADVANTAGE, BUT IT'LL HAVE TO DO.

IT'S A POSEY STRAITJACKET.

THE JOKER CLAIMED IT'S THE SAME ONE HE ESCAPED FROM LAST TIME HE WAS IN ARKHAM.

IF HE GOT OUT OF IT, I CAN.

ACTUALLY, ANYONE CAN, IF THEY'RE WILLING TO TAKE THE PAIN.

KRAK

I LIFT MY ELBOWS UP TOWARDS MY NECK UNTIL BOTH OF MY SHOULDERS DISLOCATE.

FROM THERE, IT'S EASY FOR ME TO REACH ONE OF MY HIDDEN CUTTING TOOLS.

52 SECONDS TO GET FREE. THAT'S TOO SLOW.

THAT'S SOMETHING OF A SPECIALTY OF MINE.

KRAK
KRAK

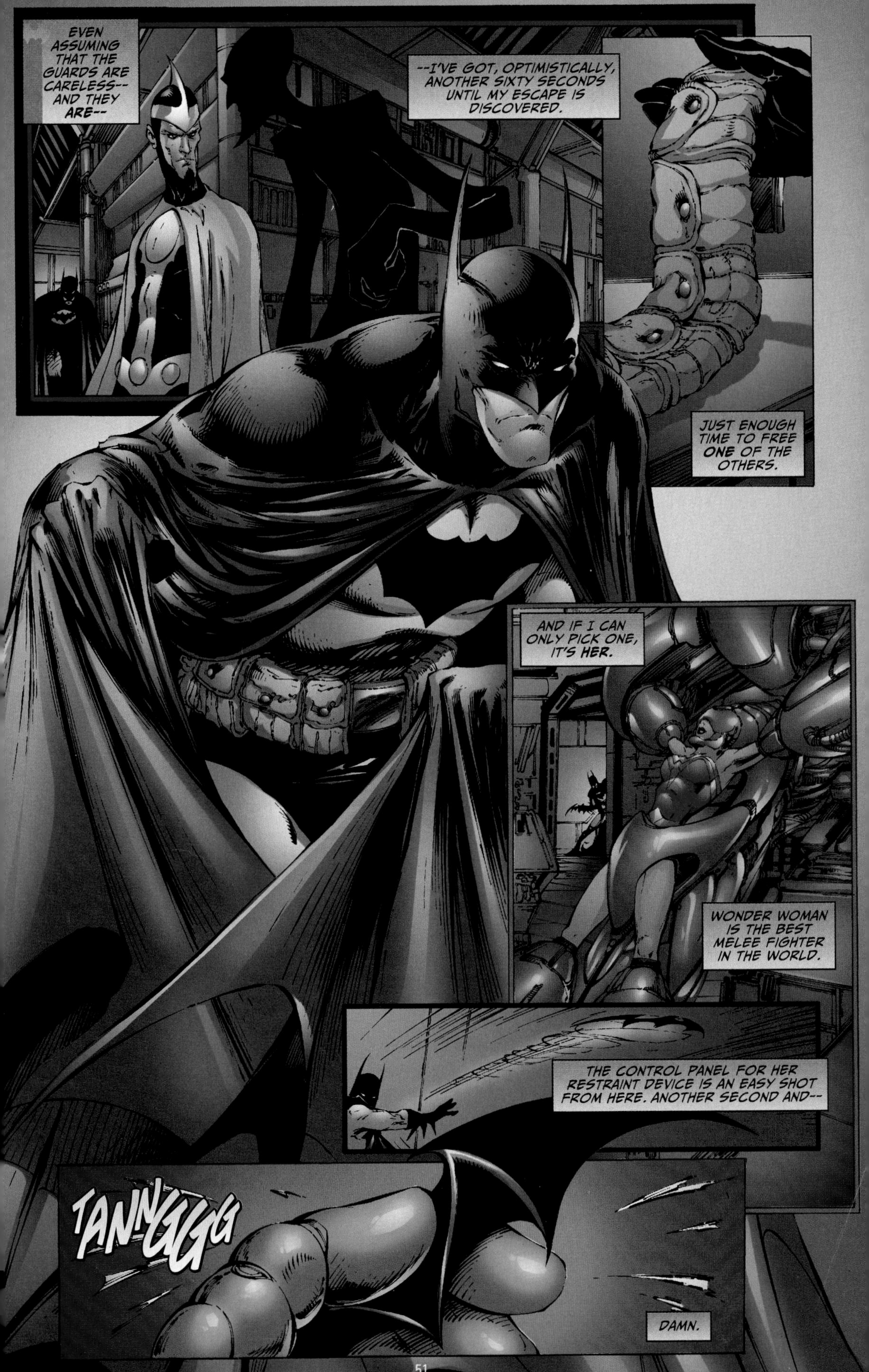
EVEN ASSUMING THAT THE GUARDS ARE CARELESS-- AND THEY ARE--
--I'VE GOT, OPTIMISTICALLY, ANOTHER SIXTY SECONDS UNTIL MY ESCAPE IS DISCOVERED.
JUST ENOUGH TIME TO FREE ONE OF THE OTHERS.
AND IF I CAN ONLY PICK ONE, IT'S HER.
WONDER WOMAN IS THE BEST MELEE FIGHTER IN THE WORLD.
THE CONTROL PANEL FOR HER RESTRAINT DEVICE IS AN EASY SHOT FROM HERE. ANOTHER SECOND AND--
TANNGGG
DAMN.

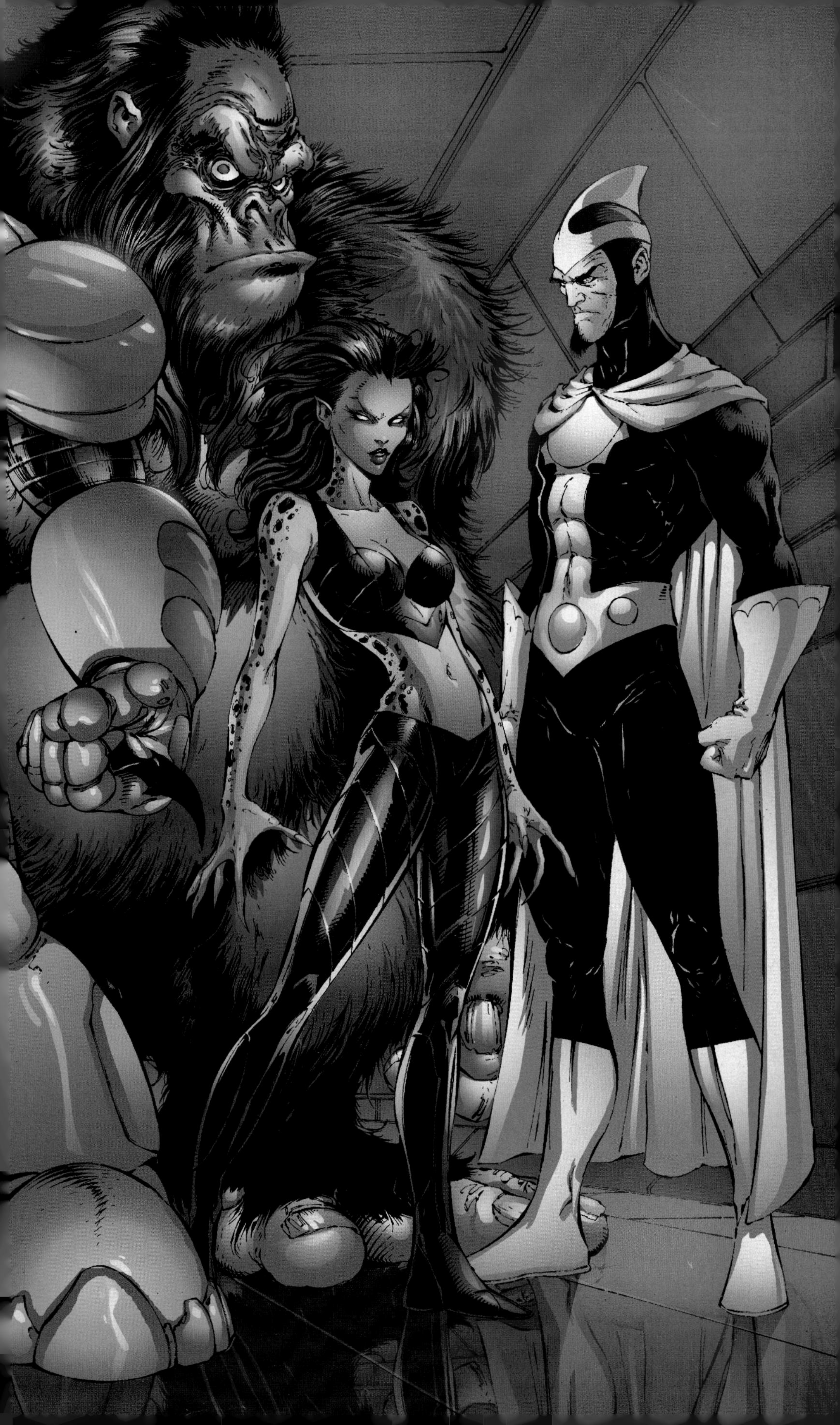

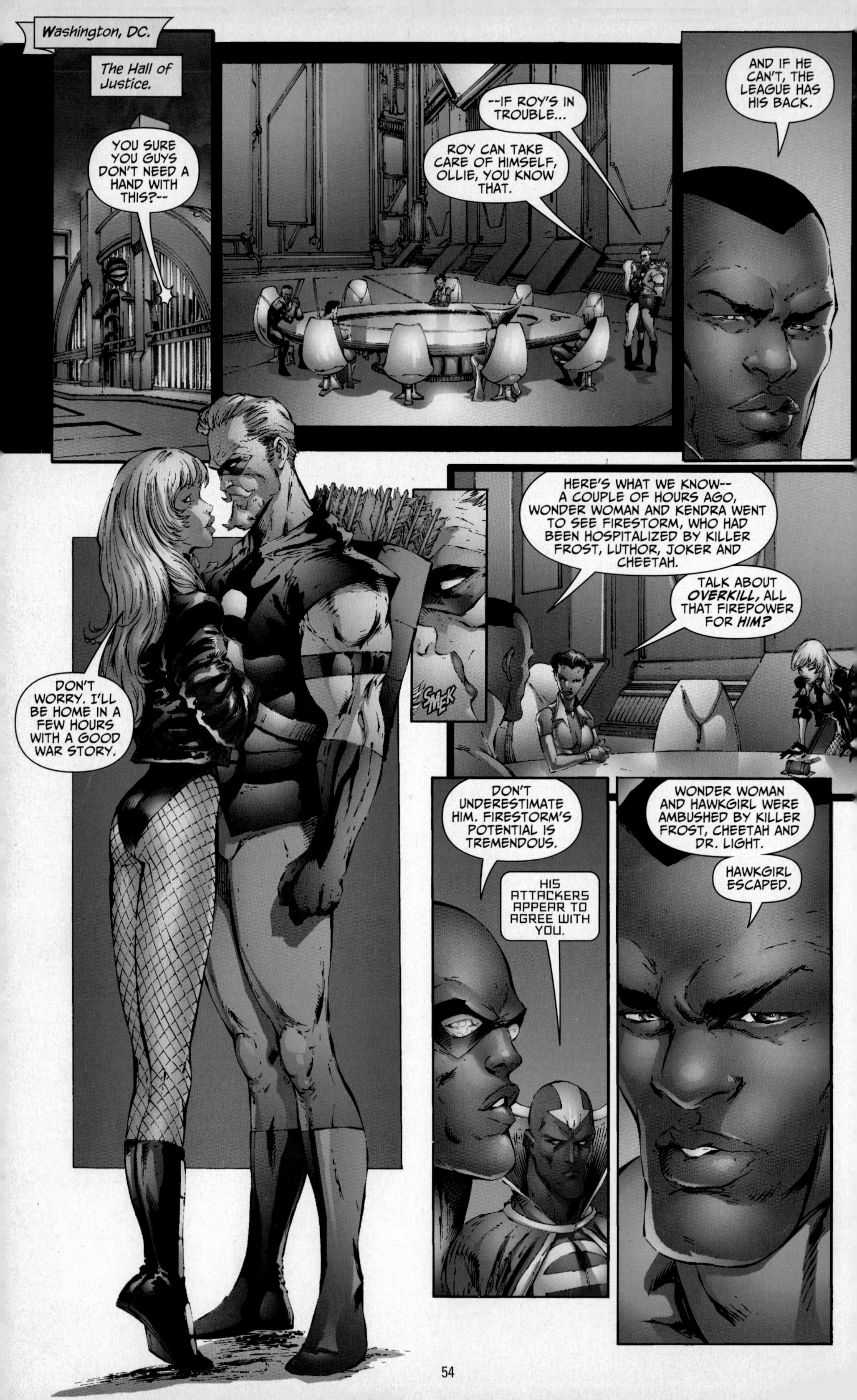
Washington, DC.
The Hall of Justice.
YOU SURE YOU GUYS DON'T NEED A HAND WITH THIS?--
--IF ROY'S IN TROUBLE...
ROY CAN TAKE CARE OF HIMSELF, OLLIE, YOU KNOW THAT.
AND IF HE CAN'T, THE LEAGUE HAS HIS BACK.
DON'T WORRY. I'LL BE HOME IN A FEW HOURS WITH A GOOD WAR STORY.
SMEK
HERE'S WHAT WE KNOW-- A COUPLE OF HOURS AGO, WONDER WOMAN AND KENDRA WENT TO SEE FIRESTORM, WHO HAD BEEN HOSPITALIZED BY KILLER FROST, LUTHOR, JOKER AND CHEETAH.
TALK ABOUT *OVERKILL,* ALL THAT FIREPOWER FOR *HIM?*
DON'T UNDERESTIMATE HIM. FIRESTORM'S POTENTIAL IS TREMENDOUS.
HIS ATTACKERS APPEAR TO AGREE WITH YOU.
WONDER WOMAN AND HAWKGIRL WERE AMBUSHED BY KILLER FROST, CHEETAH AND DR. LIGHT.
HAWKGIRL ESCAPED.

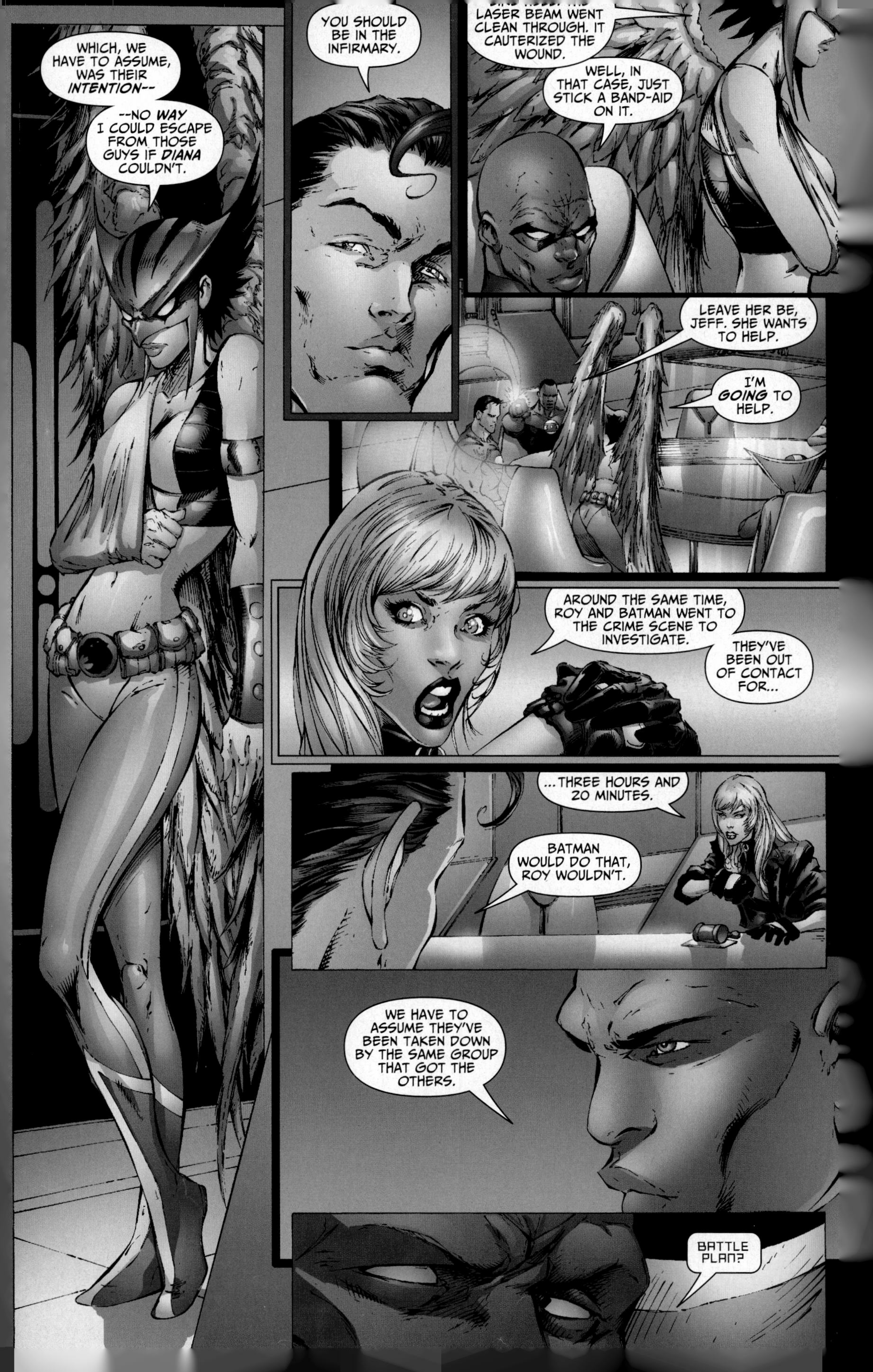
WHICH, WE HAVE TO ASSUME, WAS THEIR *INTENTION*--
--NO *WAY* I COULD ESCAPE FROM THOSE GUYS IF *DIANA* COULDN'T.
YOU SHOULD BE IN THE INFIRMARY.
LASER BEAM WENT CLEAN THROUGH. IT CAUTERIZED THE WOUND.
WELL, IN THAT CASE, JUST STICK A BAND-AID ON IT.
LEAVE HER BE, JEFF. SHE WANTS TO HELP.
I'M *GOING* TO HELP.
AROUND THE SAME TIME, ROY AND BATMAN WENT TO THE CRIME SCENE TO INVESTIGATE.
THEY'VE BEEN OUT OF CONTACT FOR...
...THREE HOURS AND 20 MINUTES.
BATMAN WOULD DO THAT, ROY WOULDN'T.
WE HAVE TO ASSUME THEY'VE BEEN TAKEN DOWN BY THE SAME GROUP THAT GOT THE OTHERS.
BATTLE PLAN?

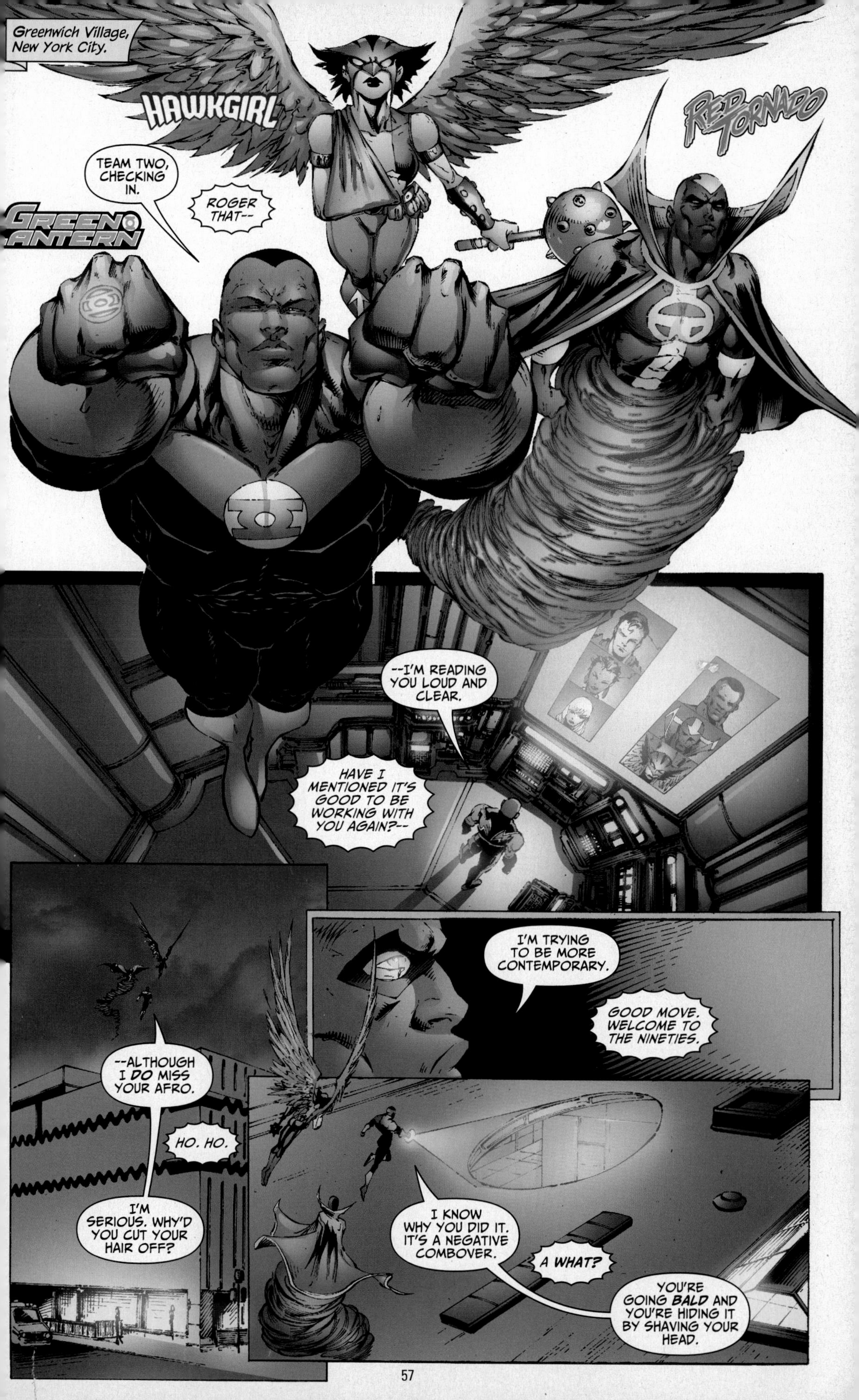

Greenwich Village, New York City.
HAWKGIRL
RED TORNADO
TEAM TWO, CHECKING IN.
GREEN LANTERN
ROGER THAT--
--I'M READING YOU LOUD AND CLEAR.
HAVE I MENTIONED IT'S GOOD TO BE WORKING WITH YOU AGAIN?--
--ALTHOUGH I DO MISS YOUR AFRO.
HO. HO.
I'M SERIOUS. WHY'D YOU CUT YOUR HAIR OFF?
I'M TRYING TO BE MORE CONTEMPORARY.
GOOD MOVE. WELCOME TO THE NINETIES.
I KNOW WHY YOU DID IT. IT'S A NEGATIVE COMBOVER.
A WHAT?
YOU'RE GOING BALD AND YOU'RE HIDING IT BY SHAVING YOUR HEAD.

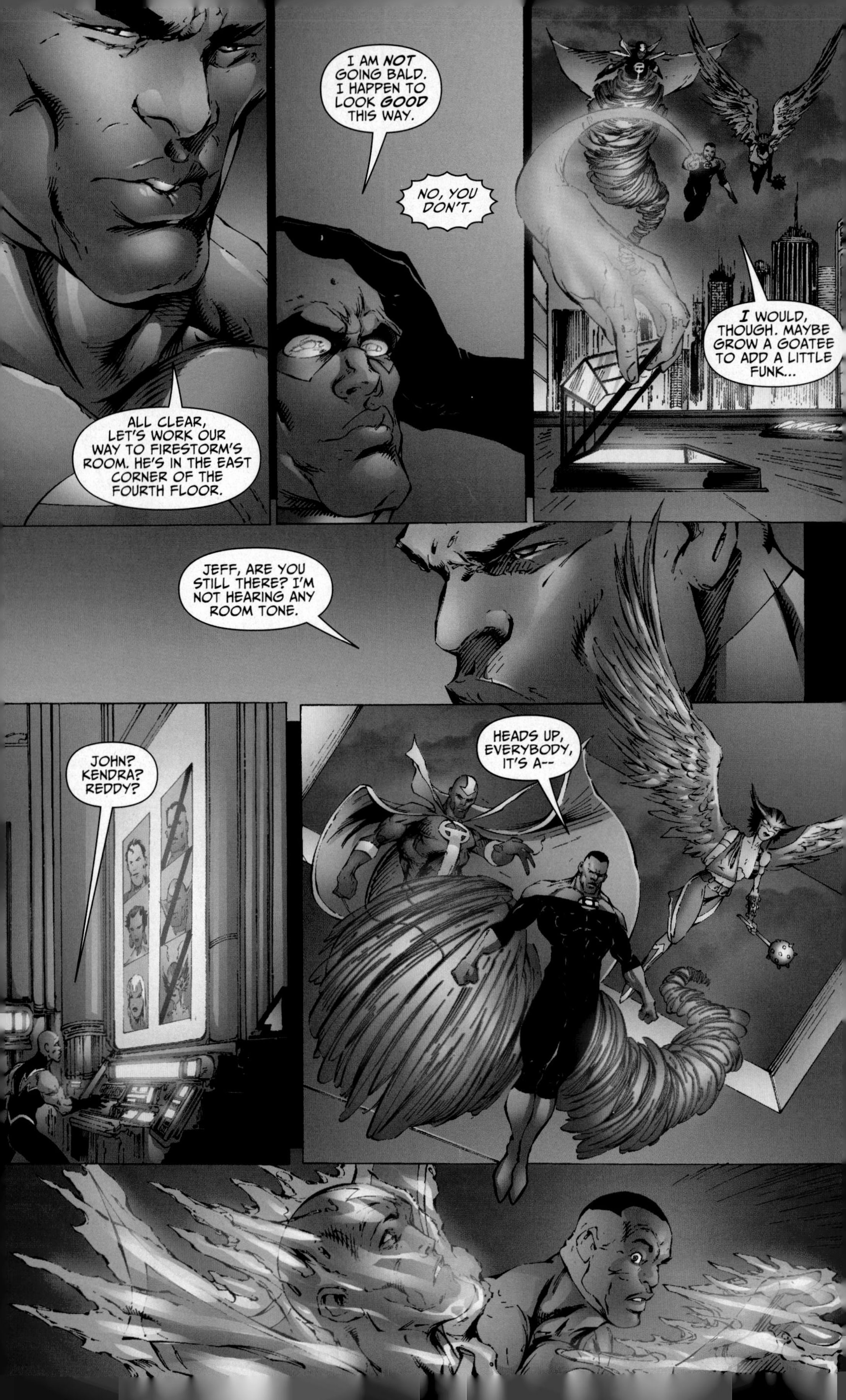
ALL CLEAR, LET'S WORK OUR WAY TO FIRESTORM'S ROOM. HE'S IN THE EAST CORNER OF THE FOURTH FLOOR.
I AM NOT GOING BALD. I HAPPEN TO LOOK GOOD THIS WAY.
NO, YOU DON'T.
I WOULD, THOUGH. MAYBE GROW A GOATEE TO ADD A LITTLE FUNK...
JEFF, ARE YOU STILL THERE? I'M NOT HEARING ANY ROOM TONE.
JOHN? KENDRA? REDDY?
HEADS UP, EVERYBODY, IT'S A--

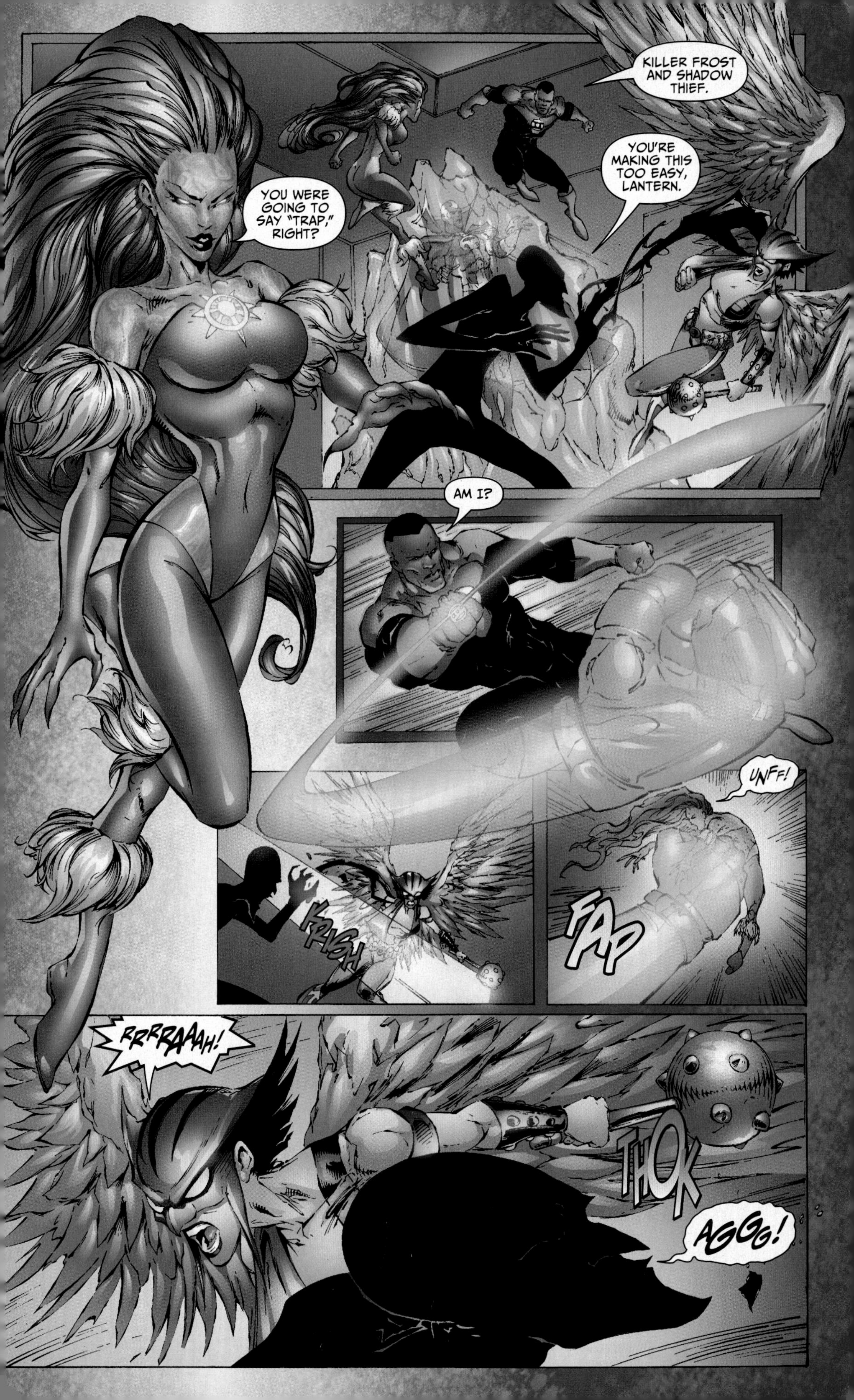
KILLER FROST AND SHADOW THIEF.
YOU WERE GOING TO SAY "TRAP," RIGHT?
YOU'RE MAKING THIS TOO EASY, LANTERN.
AM I?
UNFF!
KRIGH
FAP
RRRRAAAH!
THOK
AGGG!

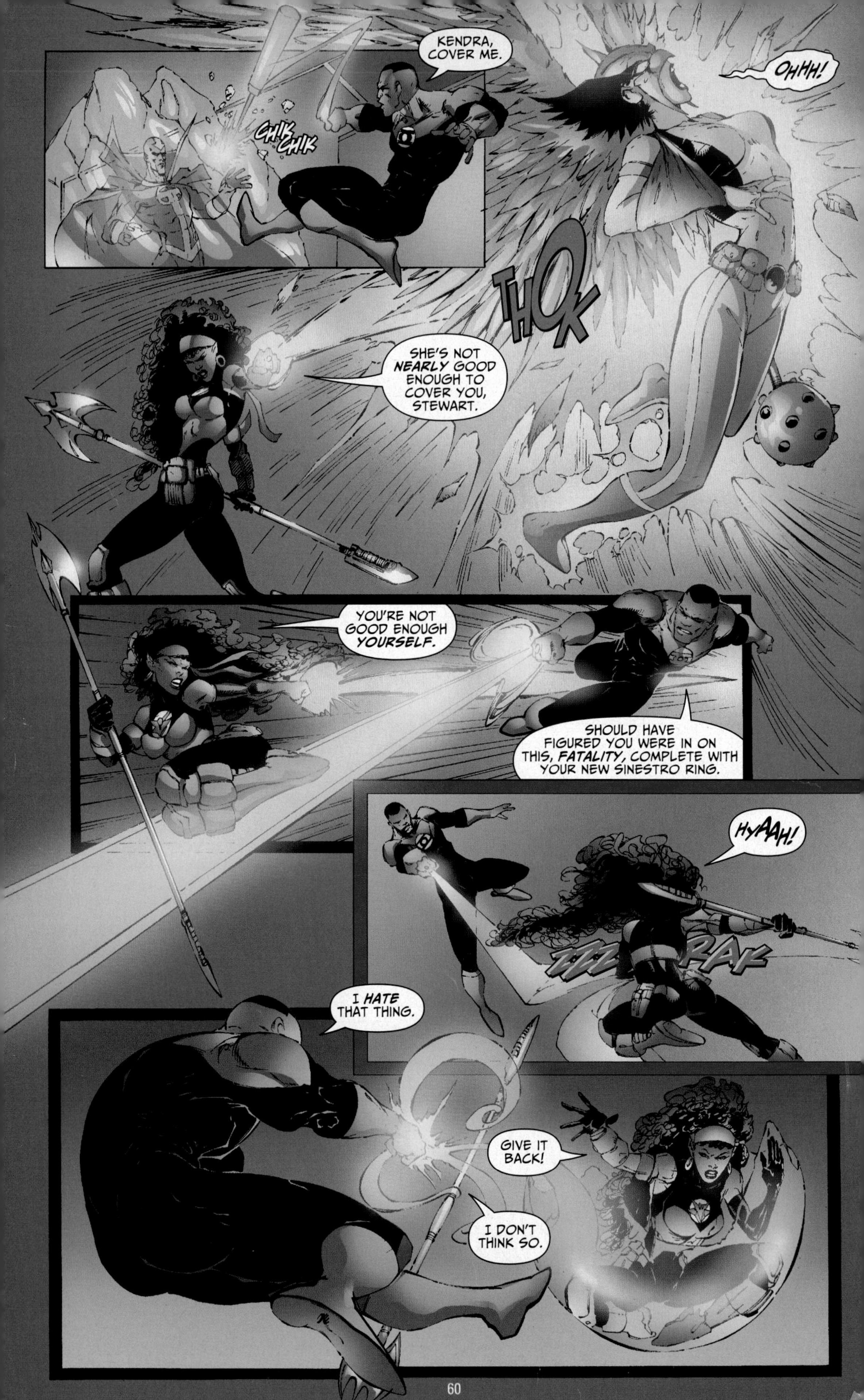

KENDRA, COVER ME.
CHIK CHIK
OHHH!
THOK
SHE'S NOT *NEARLY* GOOD ENOUGH TO COVER YOU, STEWART.
YOU'RE NOT GOOD ENOUGH *YOURSELF*.
SHOULD HAVE FIGURED YOU WERE IN ON THIS, *FATALITY*, COMPLETE WITH YOUR NEW SINESTRO RING.
HYAAH!
ZZZRAK
I *HATE* THAT THING.
GIVE IT BACK!
I DON'T THINK SO.

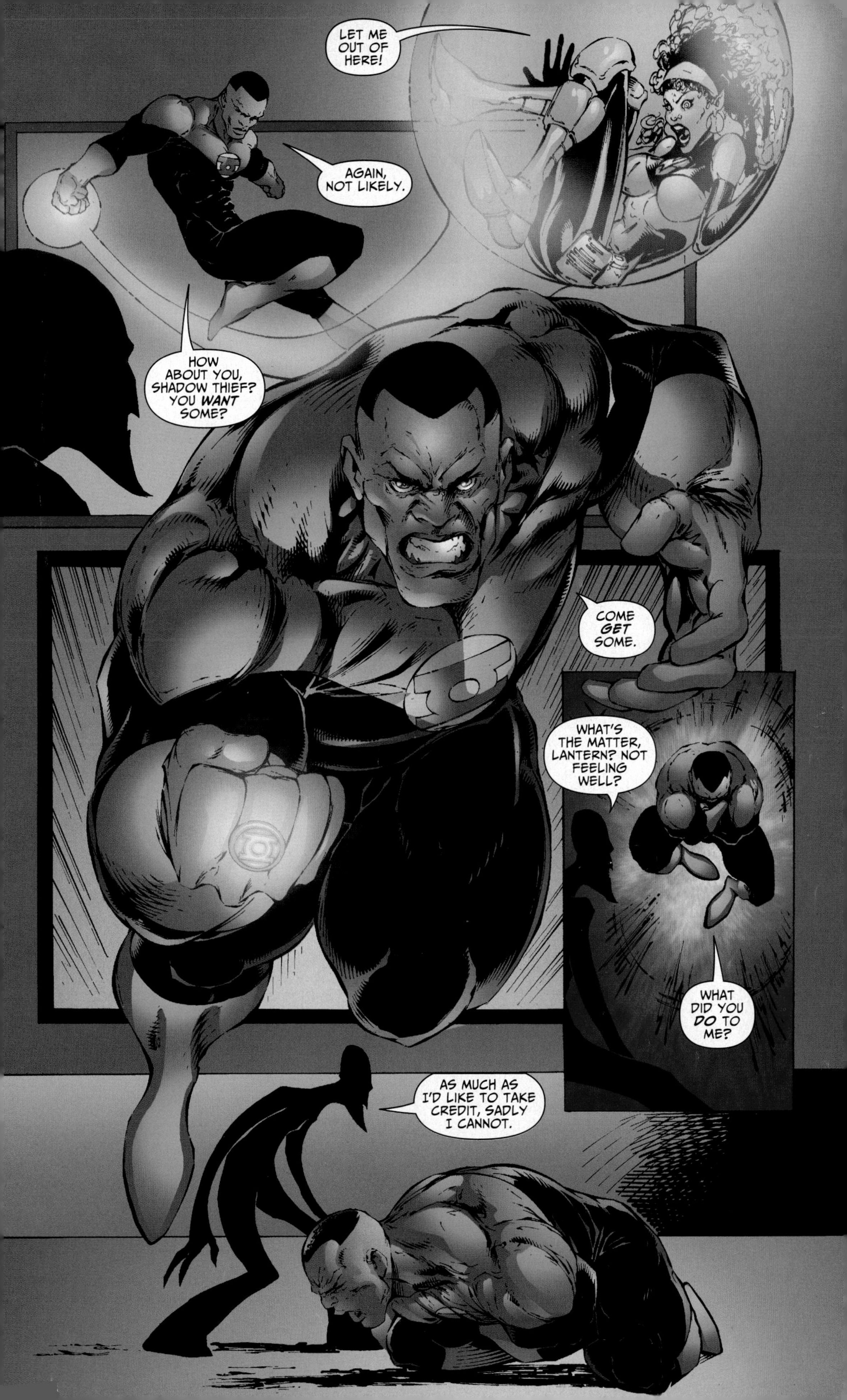
LET ME OUT OF HERE!
AGAIN, NOT LIKELY.
HOW ABOUT YOU, SHADOW THIEF? YOU **WANT** SOME?
COME **GET** SOME.
WHAT'S THE MATTER, LANTERN? NOT FEELING WELL?
WHAT DID YOU **DO** TO ME?
AS MUCH AS I'D LIKE TO TAKE CREDIT, SADLY I CANNOT.

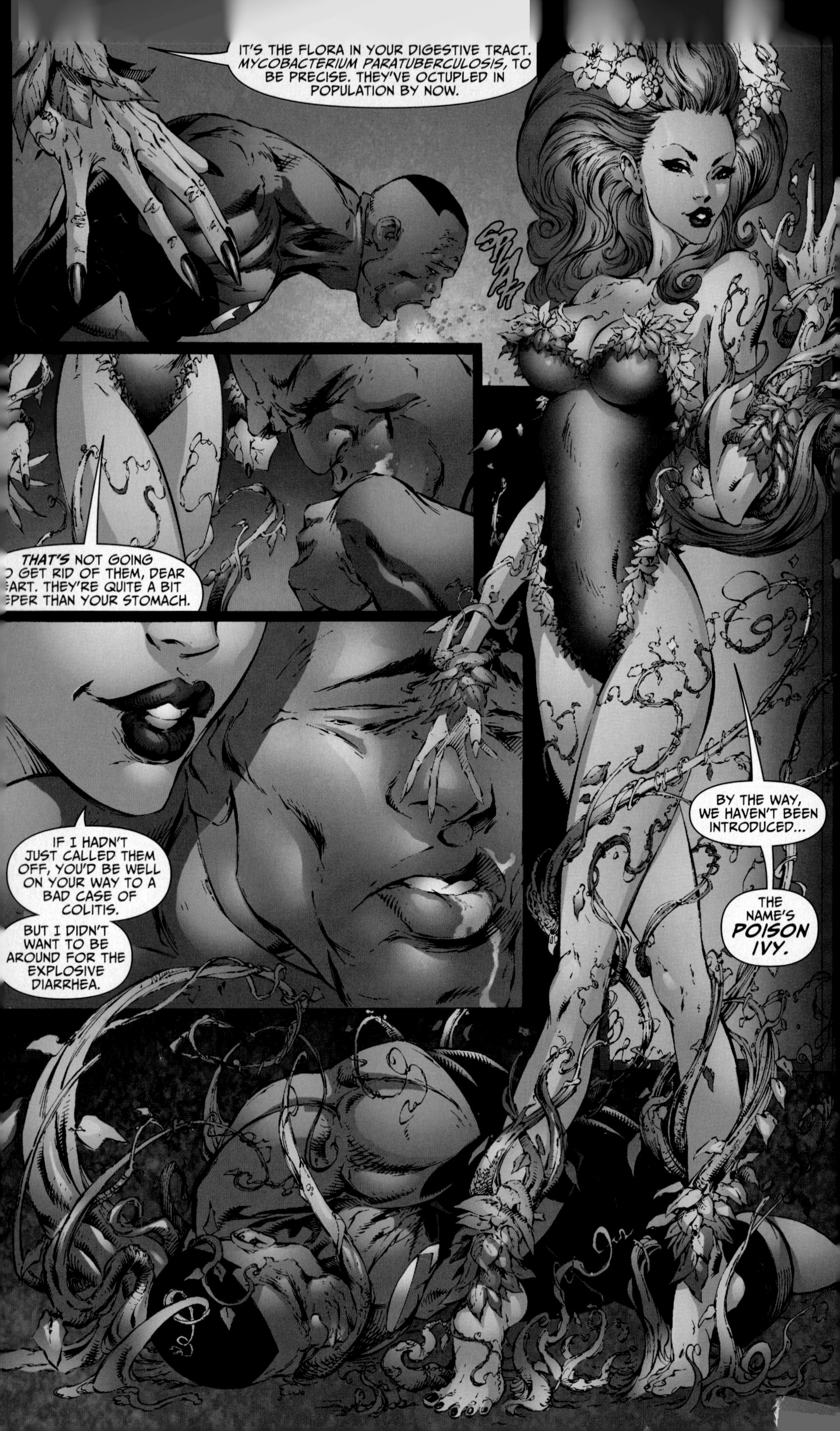
IT'S THE FLORA IN YOUR DIGESTIVE TRACT. *MYCOBACTERIUM PARATUBERCULOSIS*, TO BE PRECISE. THEY'VE OCTUPLED IN POPULATION BY NOW.
THAT'S NOT GOING O GET RID OF THEM, DEAR EART. THEY'RE QUITE A BIT EPER THAN YOUR STOMACH.
IF I HADN'T JUST CALLED THEM OFF, YOU'D BE WELL ON YOUR WAY TO A BAD CASE OF COLITIS.
BUT I DIDN'T WANT TO BE AROUND FOR THE EXPLOSIVE DIARRHEA.
BY THE WAY, WE HAVEN'T BEEN INTRODUCED...
THE NAME'S ***POISON IVY.***

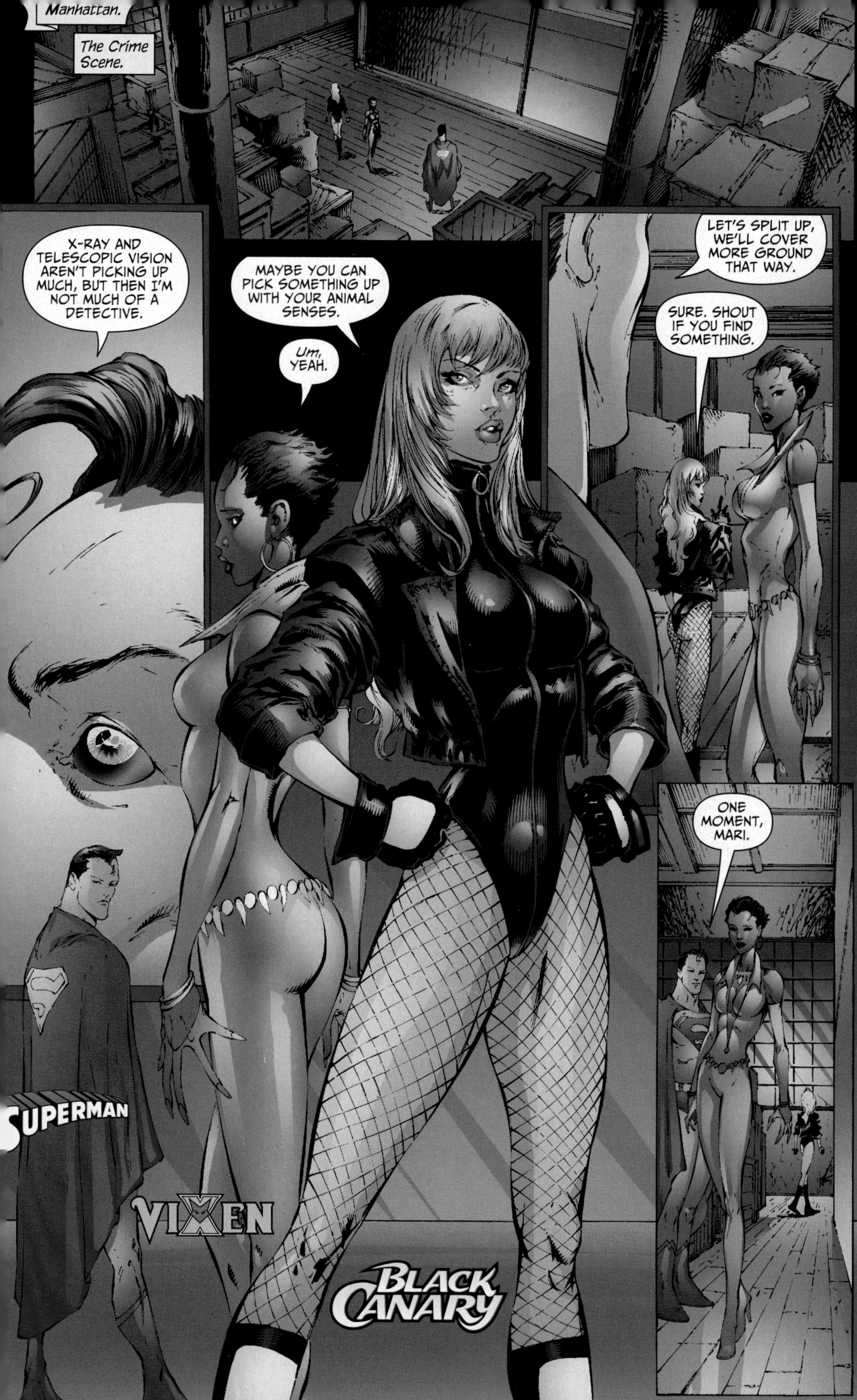
Manhattan.
The Crime Scene.
X-RAY AND TELESCOPIC VISION AREN'T PICKING UP MUCH, BUT THEN I'M NOT MUCH OF A DETECTIVE.
MAYBE YOU CAN PICK SOMETHING UP WITH YOUR ANIMAL SENSES.
Um, YEAH.
LET'S SPLIT UP, WE'LL COVER MORE GROUND THAT WAY.
SURE. SHOUT IF YOU FIND SOMETHING.
ONE MOMENT, MARI.
SUPERMAN
VIXEN
BLACK CANARY

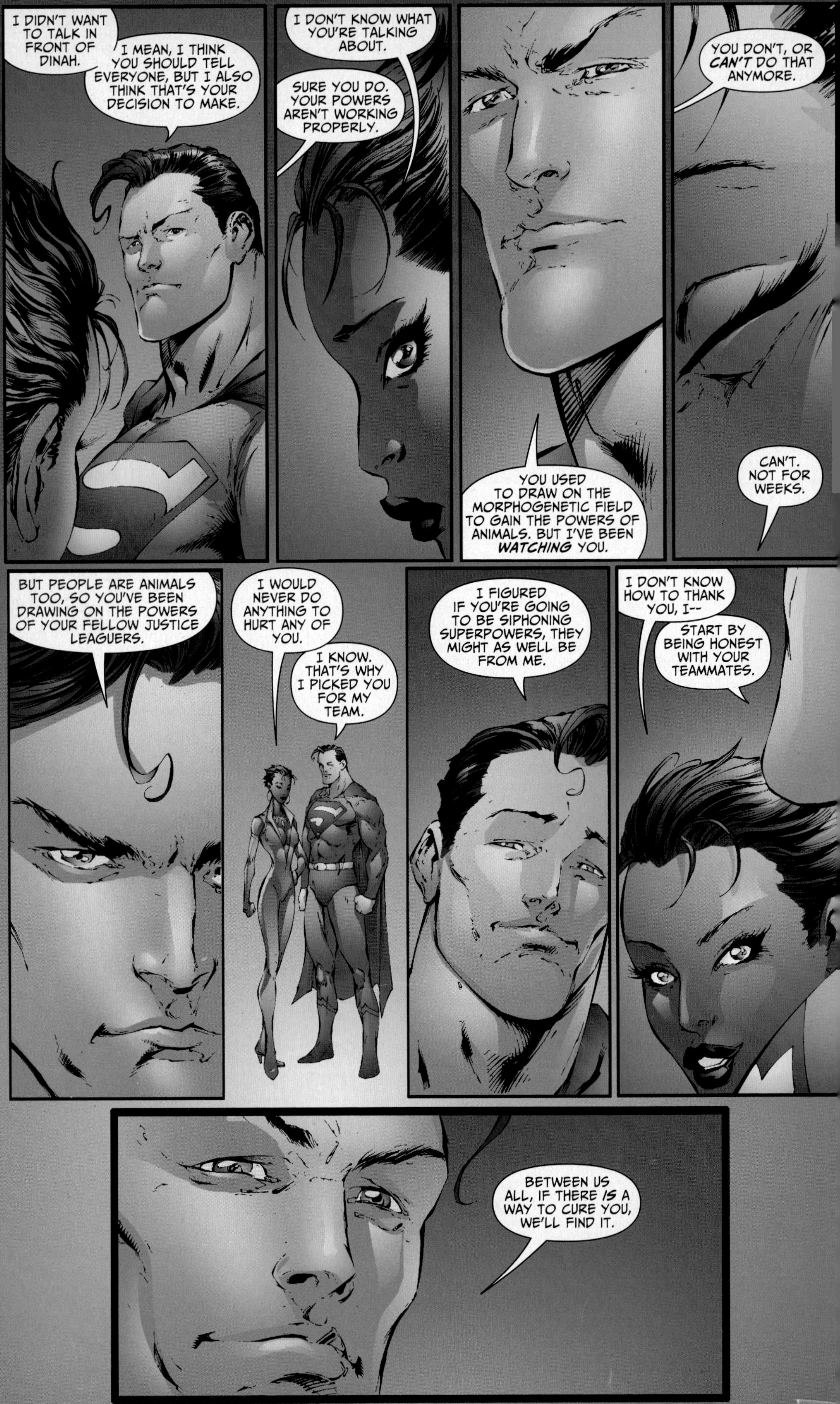

I DIDN'T WANT TO TALK IN FRONT OF DINAH.
I MEAN, I THINK YOU SHOULD TELL EVERYONE, BUT I ALSO THINK THAT'S YOUR DECISION TO MAKE.
I DON'T KNOW WHAT YOU'RE TALKING ABOUT.
SURE YOU DO. YOUR POWERS AREN'T WORKING PROPERLY.
YOU USED TO DRAW ON THE MORPHOGENETIC FIELD TO GAIN THE POWERS OF ANIMALS. BUT I'VE BEEN *WATCHING* YOU.
YOU DON'T, OR *CAN'T* DO THAT ANYMORE.
CAN'T. NOT FOR WEEKS.
BUT PEOPLE ARE ANIMALS TOO, SO YOU'VE BEEN DRAWING ON THE POWERS OF YOUR FELLOW JUSTICE LEAGUERS.
I WOULD NEVER DO ANYTHING TO HURT ANY OF YOU.
I KNOW. THAT'S WHY I PICKED YOU FOR MY TEAM.
I FIGURED IF YOU'RE GOING TO BE SIPHONING SUPERPOWERS, THEY MIGHT AS WELL BE FROM ME.
I DON'T KNOW HOW TO THANK YOU, I--
START BY BEING HONEST WITH YOUR TEAMMATES.
BETWEEN US ALL, IF THERE *IS* A WAY TO CURE YOU, WE'LL FIND IT.

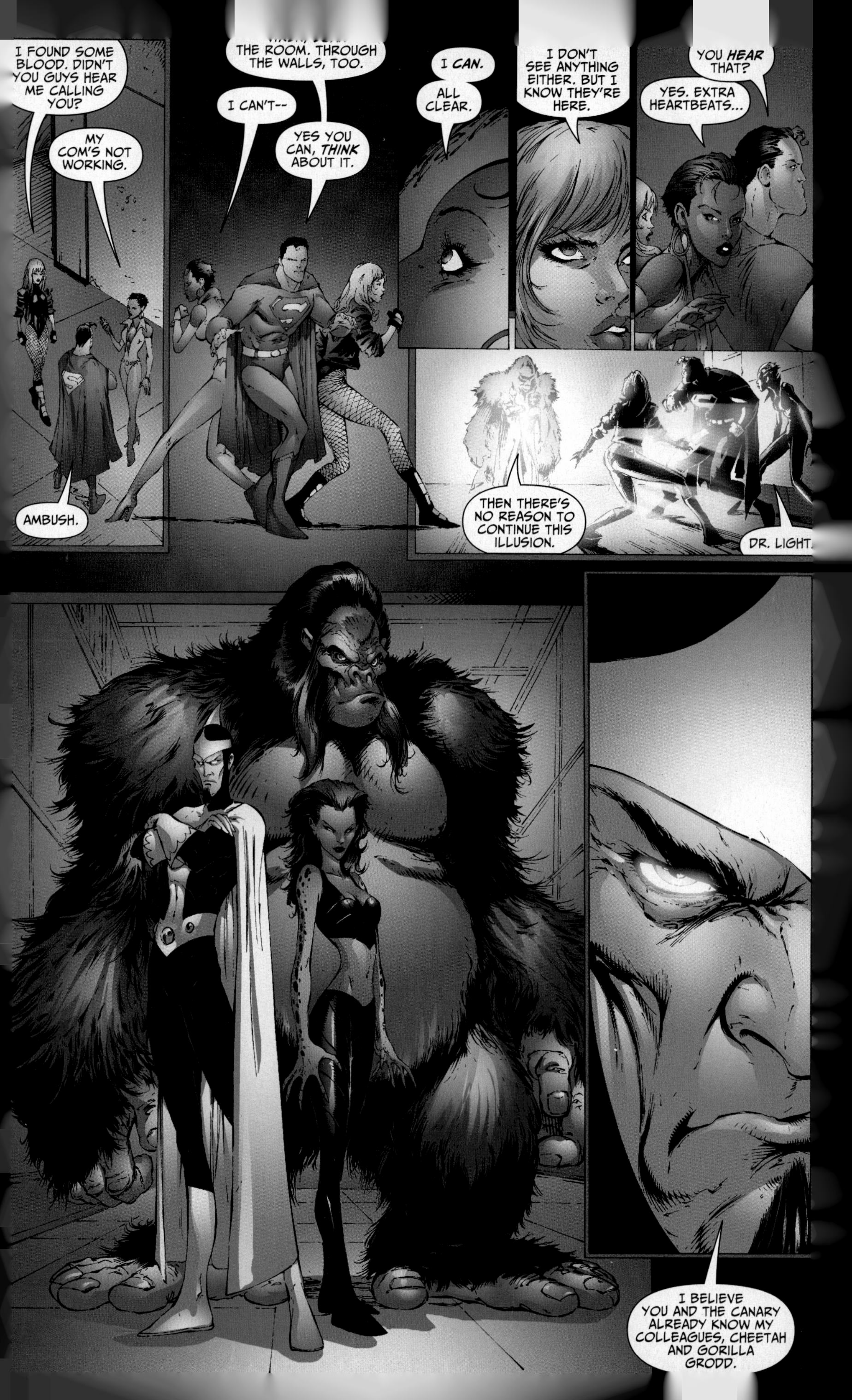

I FOUND SOME BLOOD. DIDN'T YOU GUYS HEAR ME CALLING YOU?
MY COM'S NOT WORKING.
AMBUSH.
THE ROOM. THROUGH THE WALLS, TOO.
I CAN'T--
YES YOU CAN, *THINK* ABOUT IT.
I *CAN.*
ALL CLEAR.
I DON'T SEE ANYTHING EITHER. BUT I KNOW THEY'RE HERE.
YOU *HEAR* THAT?
YES. EXTRA HEARTBEATS...
THEN THERE'S NO REASON TO CONTINUE THIS ILLUSION.
DR. LIGHT.
I BELIEVE YOU AND THE CANARY ALREADY KNOW MY COLLEAGUES, CHEETAH AND GORILLA GRODD.

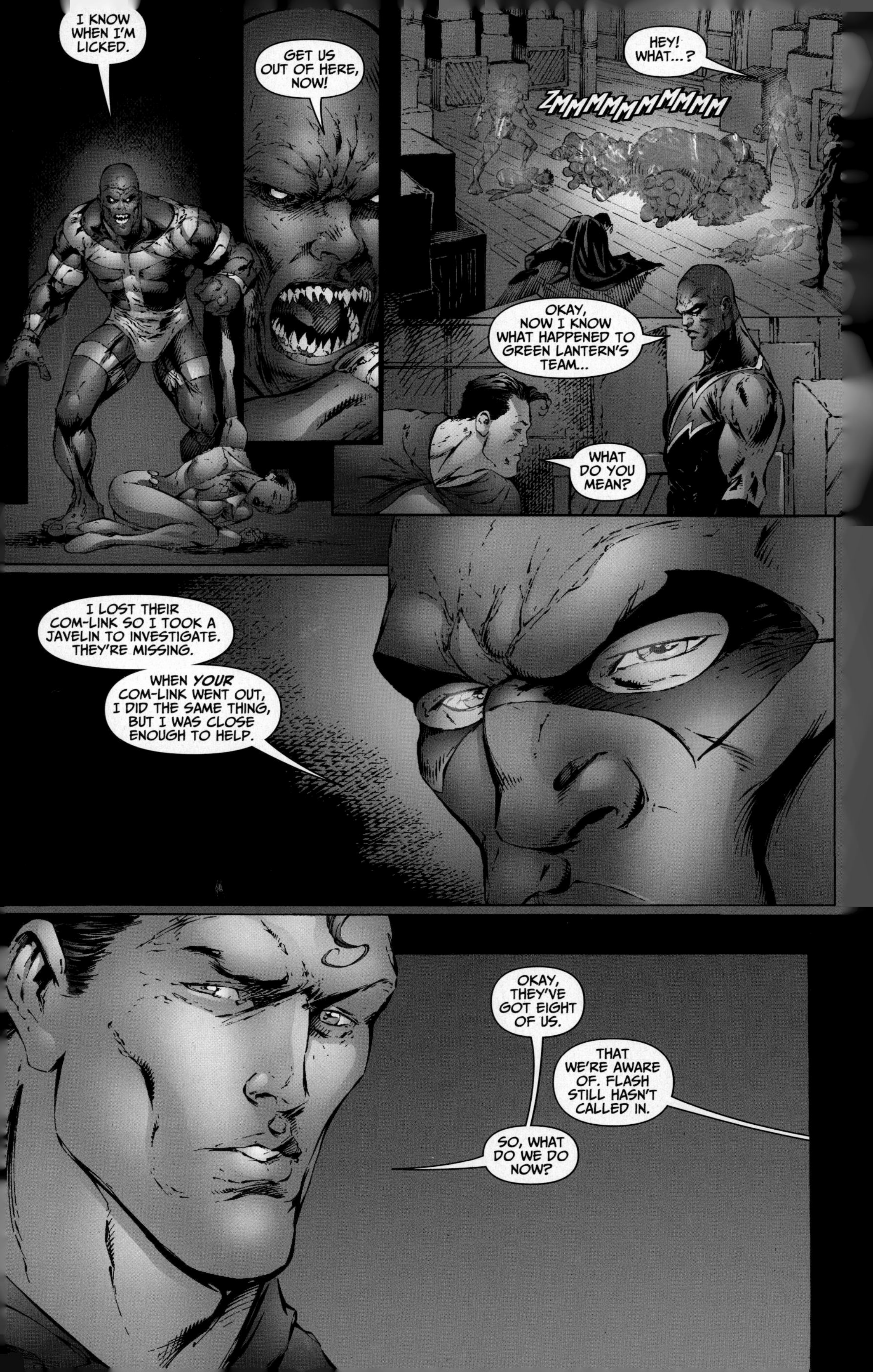

I KNOW WHEN I'M LICKED.
GET US OUT OF HERE, NOW!
HEY! WHAT...?
ZMMMMMMMMMM
OKAY, NOW I KNOW WHAT HAPPENED TO GREEN LANTERN'S TEAM...
WHAT DO YOU MEAN?
I LOST THEIR COM-LINK SO I TOOK A JAVELIN TO INVESTIGATE. THEY'RE MISSING.
WHEN *YOUR* COM-LINK WENT OUT, I DID THE SAME THING, BUT I WAS CLOSE ENOUGH TO HELP.
OKAY, THEY'VE GOT EIGHT OF US.
THAT WE'RE AWARE OF. FLASH STILL HASN'T CALLED IN.
SO, WHAT DO WE DO NOW?

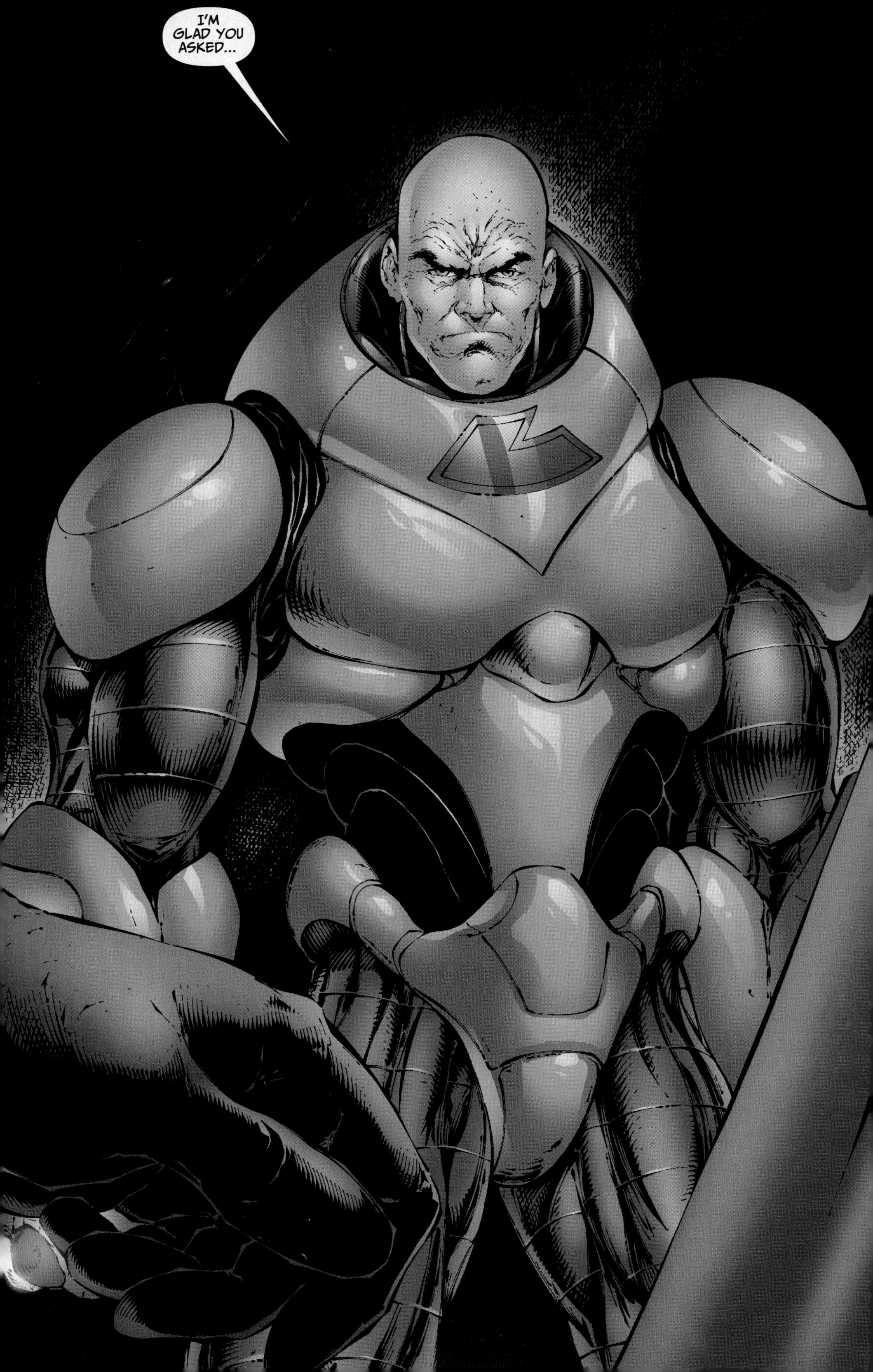
I'M GLAD YOU ASKED...

COVER ART BY IAN CHURCHILL & NORM RAPMUND WITH ALEX SINCLAIR

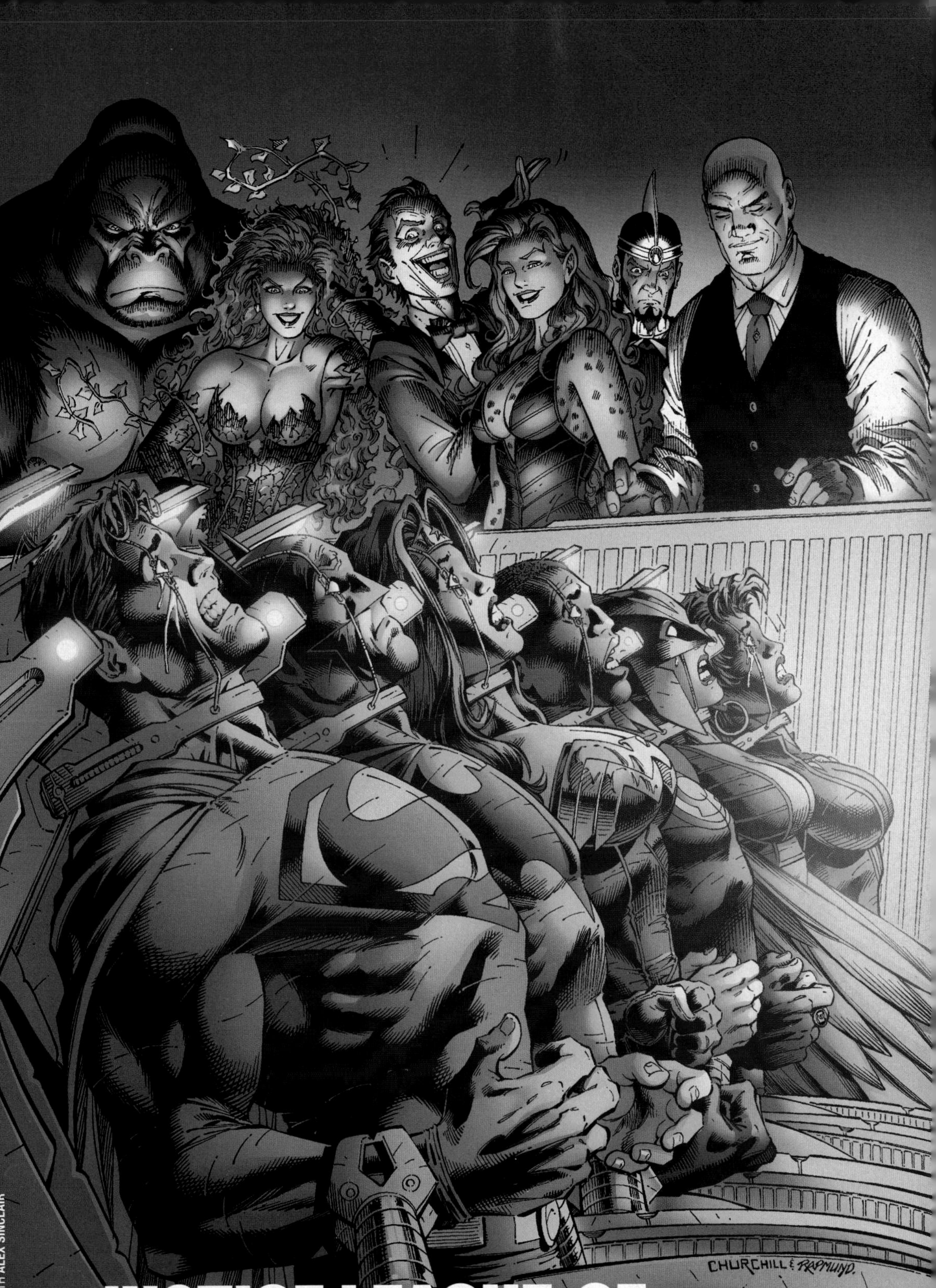
CHURCHILL & RAPMUND.

JUSTICE LEAGUE OF AMERICA
CHAPTER THREE

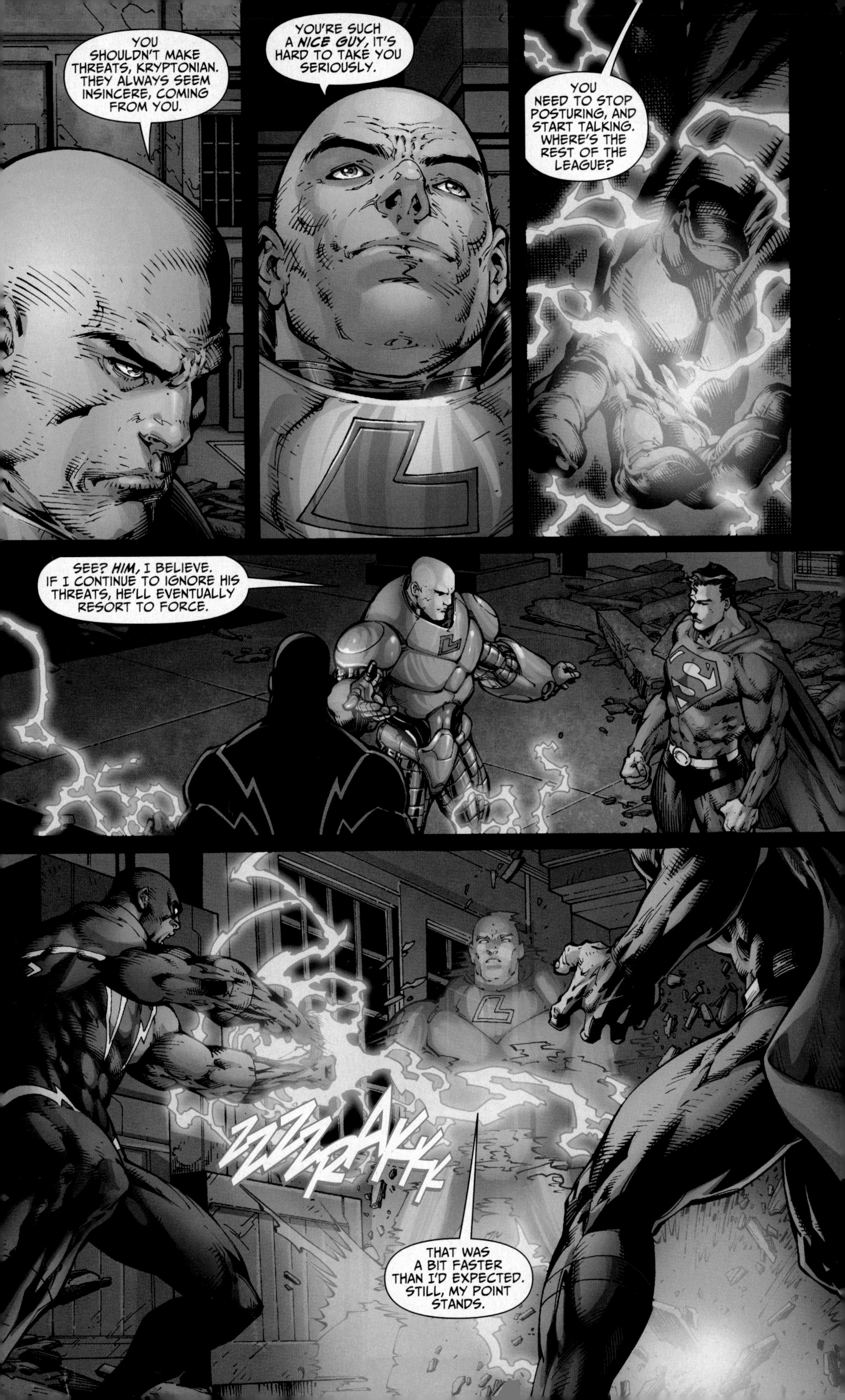
YOU SHOULDN'T MAKE THREATS, KRYPTONIAN. THEY ALWAYS SEEM INSINCERE, COMING FROM YOU.
YOU'RE SUCH A NICE GUY, IT'S HARD TO TAKE YOU SERIOUSLY.
YOU NEED TO STOP POSTURING, AND START TALKING. WHERE'S THE REST OF THE LEAGUE?
SEE? HIM, I BELIEVE. IF I CONTINUE TO IGNORE HIS THREATS, HE'LL EVENTUALLY RESORT TO FORCE.
ZZZZRAKKK
THAT WAS A BIT FASTER THAN I'D EXPECTED. STILL, MY POINT STANDS.

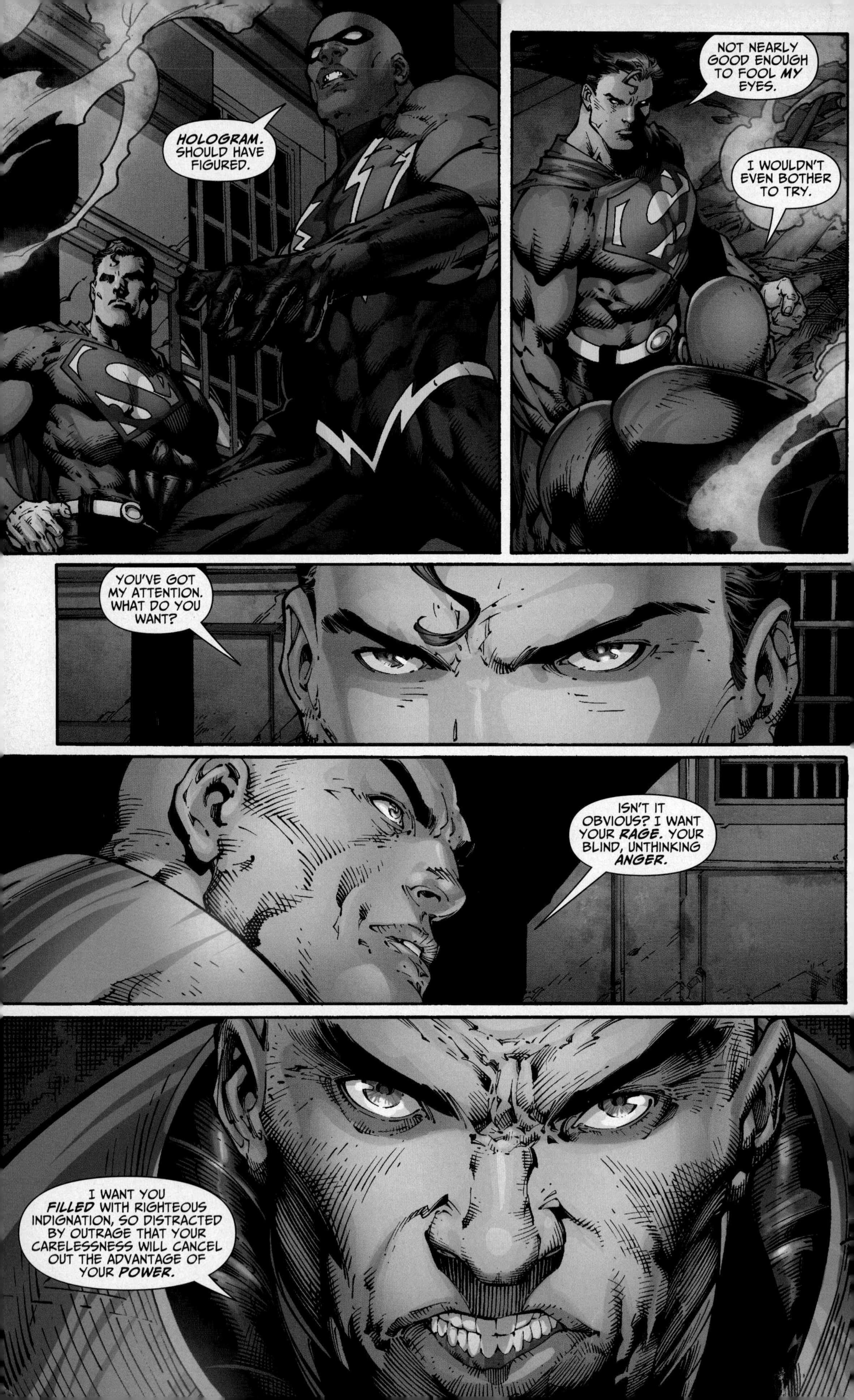
HOLOGRAM. SHOULD HAVE FIGURED.
NOT NEARLY GOOD ENOUGH TO FOOL MY EYES.
I WOULDN'T EVEN BOTHER TO TRY.
YOU'VE GOT MY ATTENTION. WHAT DO YOU WANT?
ISN'T IT OBVIOUS? I WANT YOUR RAGE. YOUR BLIND, UNTHINKING ANGER.
I WANT YOU FILLED WITH RIGHTEOUS INDIGNATION, SO DISTRACTED BY OUTRAGE THAT YOUR CARELESSNESS WILL CANCEL OUT THE ADVANTAGE OF YOUR POWER.

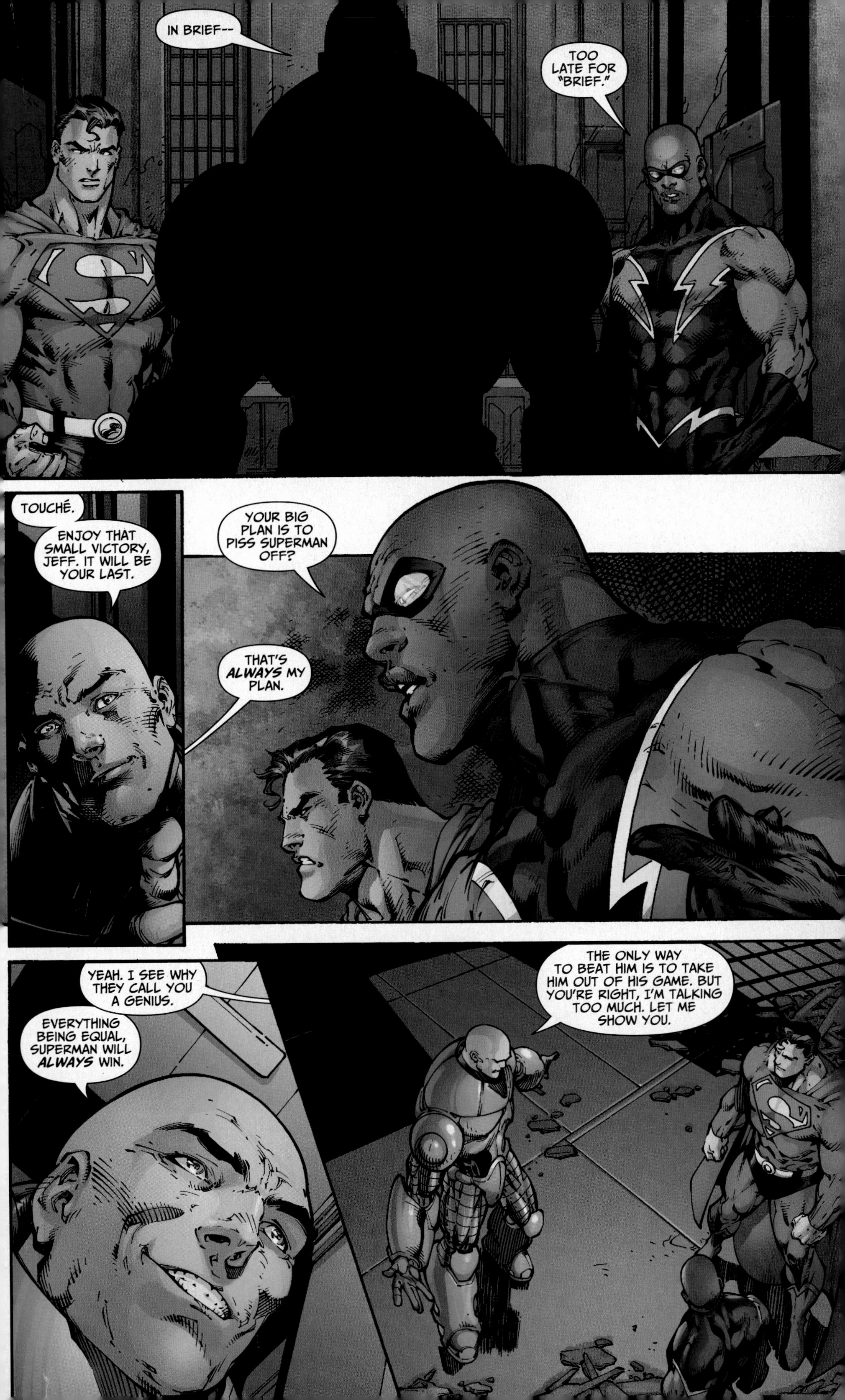
IN BRIEF--
TOO LATE FOR "BRIEF."
TOUCHÉ.
ENJOY THAT SMALL VICTORY, JEFF. IT WILL BE YOUR LAST.
YOUR BIG PLAN IS TO PISS SUPERMAN OFF?
THAT'S *ALWAYS* MY PLAN.
YEAH. I SEE WHY THEY CALL YOU A GENIUS.
EVERYTHING BEING EQUAL, SUPERMAN WILL *ALWAYS* WIN.
THE ONLY WAY TO BEAT HIM IS TO TAKE HIM OUT OF HIS GAME. BUT YOU'RE RIGHT, I'M TALKING TOO MUCH. LET ME SHOW YOU.

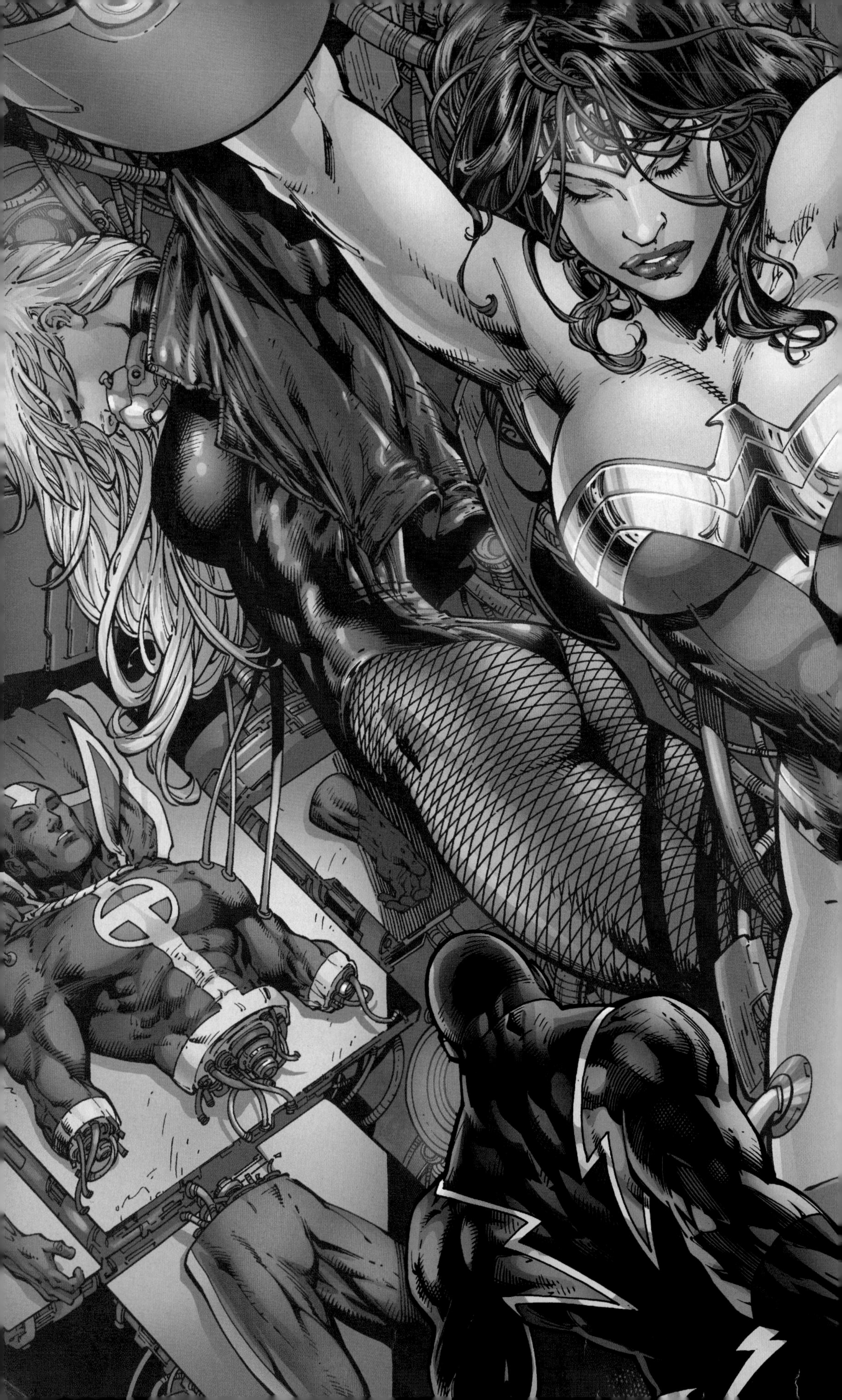

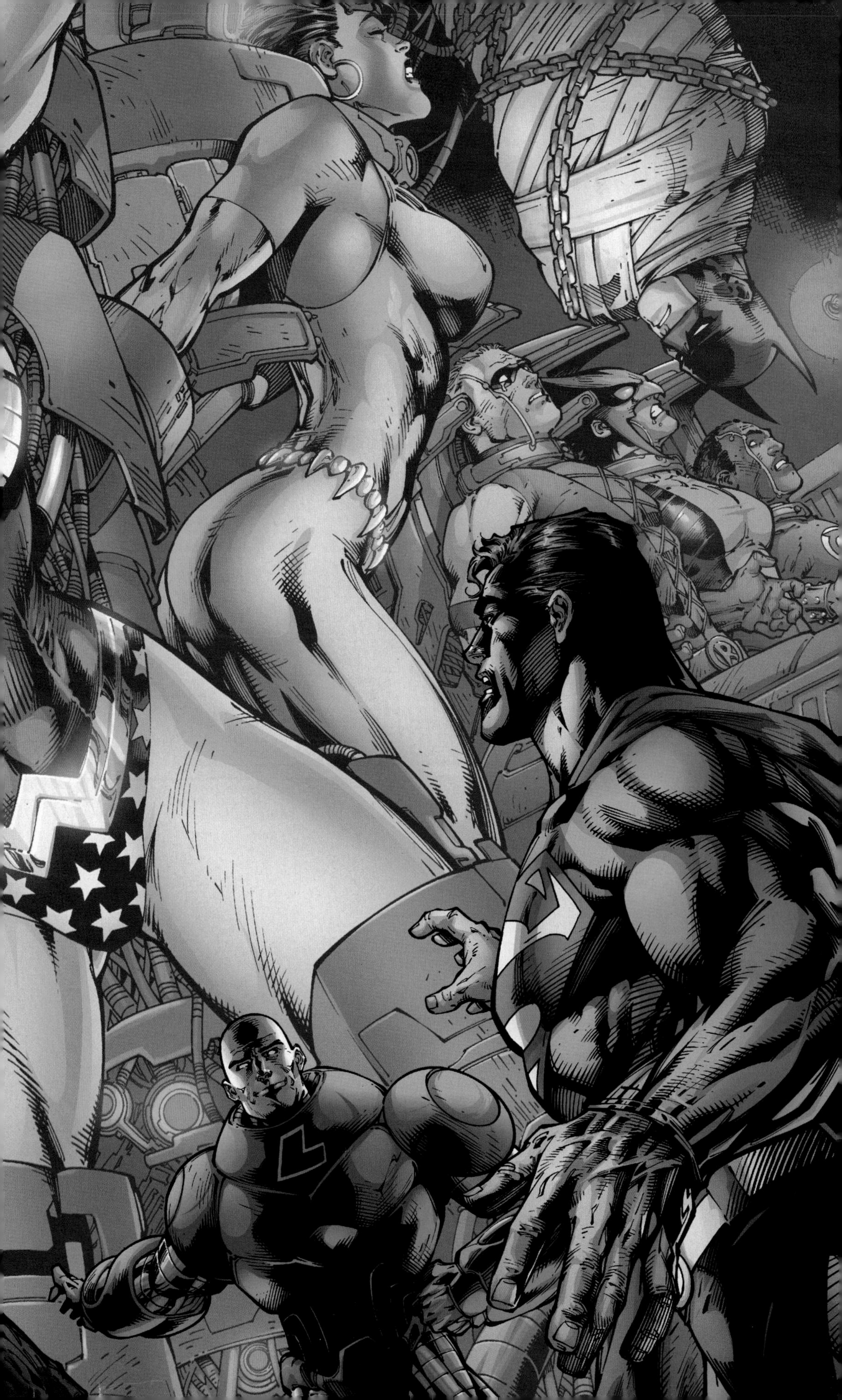

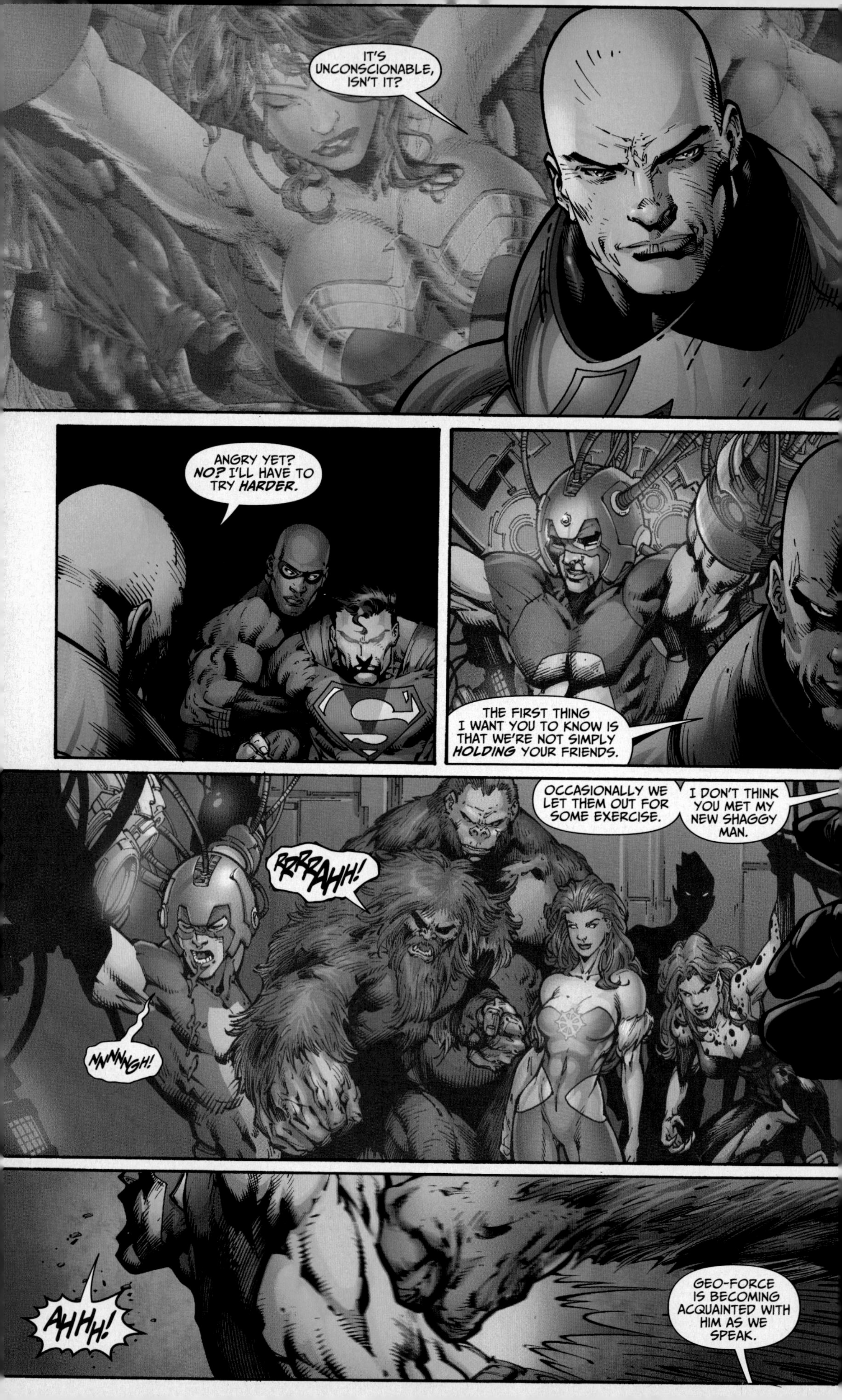
IT'S UNCONSCIONABLE, ISN'T IT?
ANGRY YET? NO? I'LL HAVE TO TRY HARDER.
THE FIRST THING I WANT YOU TO KNOW IS THAT WE'RE NOT SIMPLY HOLDING YOUR FRIENDS.
OCCASIONALLY WE LET THEM OUT FOR SOME EXERCISE.
I DON'T THINK YOU MET MY NEW SHAGGY MAN.
RRRRAHH!
NNNNNGH!
AHHH!
GEO-FORCE IS BECOMING ACQUAINTED WITH HIM AS WE SPEAK.

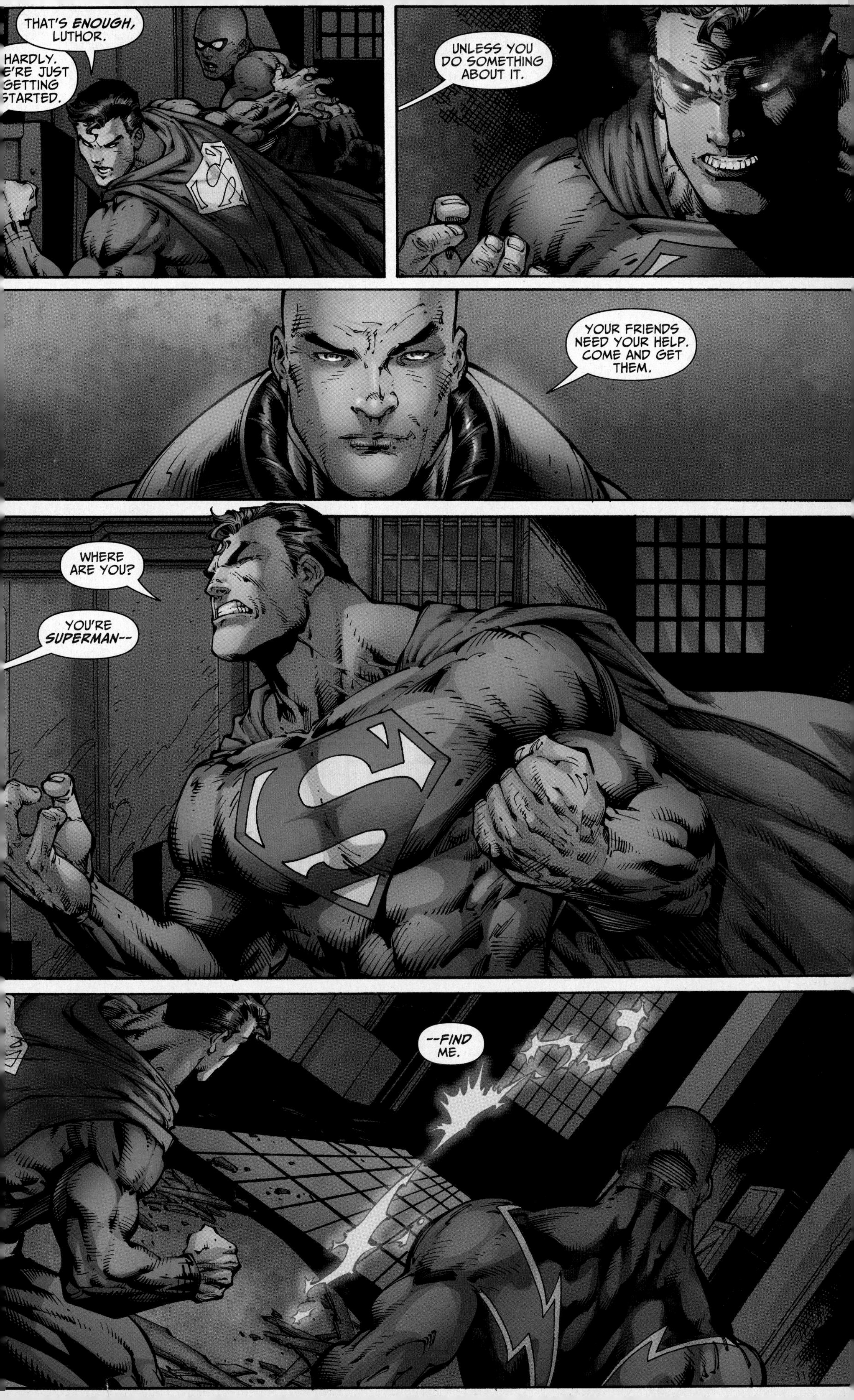

THAT'S ENOUGH, LUTHOR.
HARDLY. WE'RE JUST GETTING STARTED.
UNLESS YOU DO SOMETHING ABOUT IT.
YOUR FRIENDS NEED YOUR HELP. COME AND GET THEM.
WHERE ARE YOU?
YOU'RE SUPERMAN--
--FIND ME.

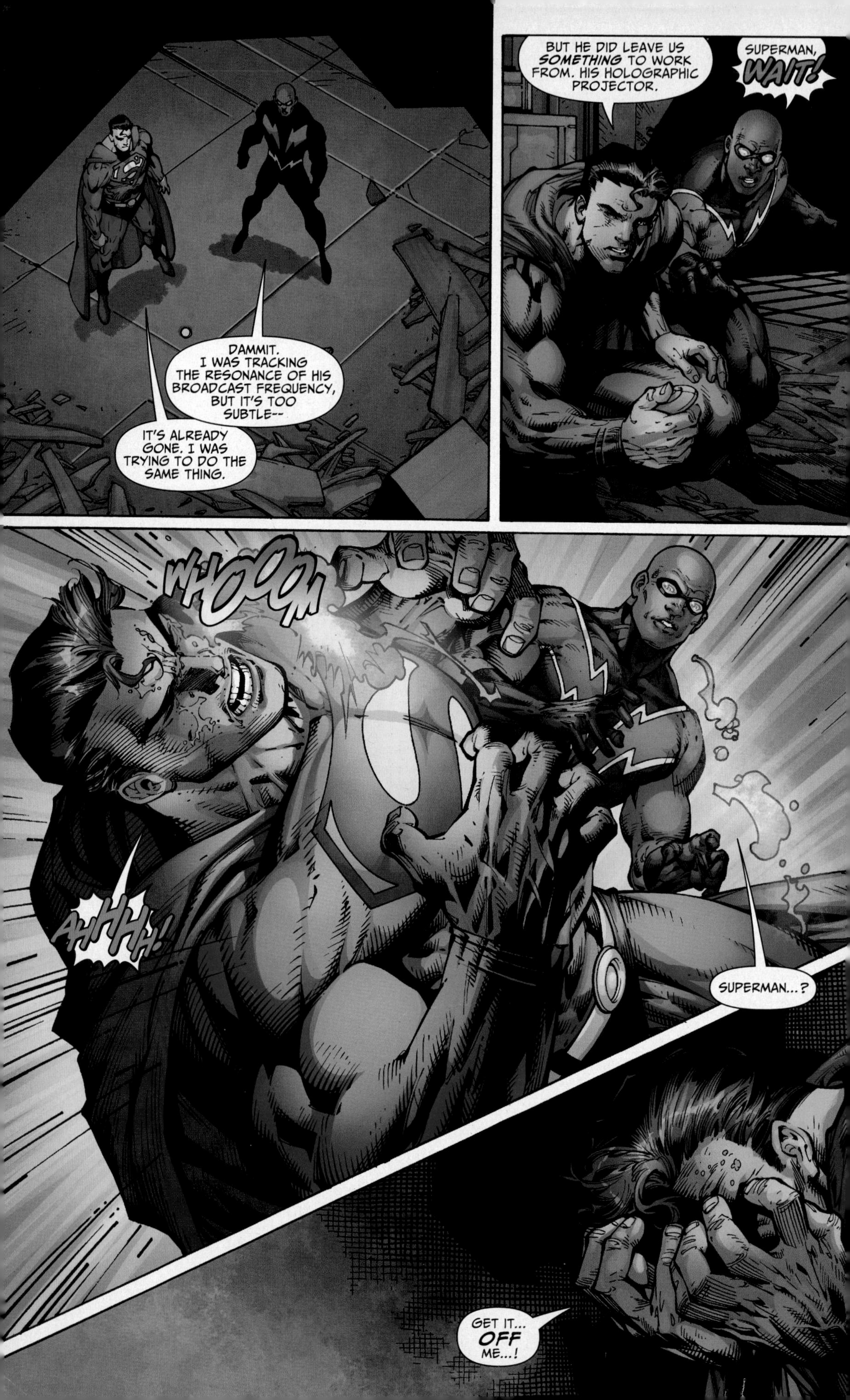
DAMMIT. I WAS TRACKING THE RESONANCE OF HIS BROADCAST FREQUENCY, BUT IT'S TOO SUBTLE--
IT'S ALREADY GONE. I WAS TRYING TO DO THE SAME THING.
BUT HE DID LEAVE US *SOMETHING* TO WORK FROM. HIS HOLOGRAPHIC PROJECTOR.
SUPERMAN, WAIT!
WHOOOM
AHHHH!
SUPERMAN...?
GET IT... OFF ME...!

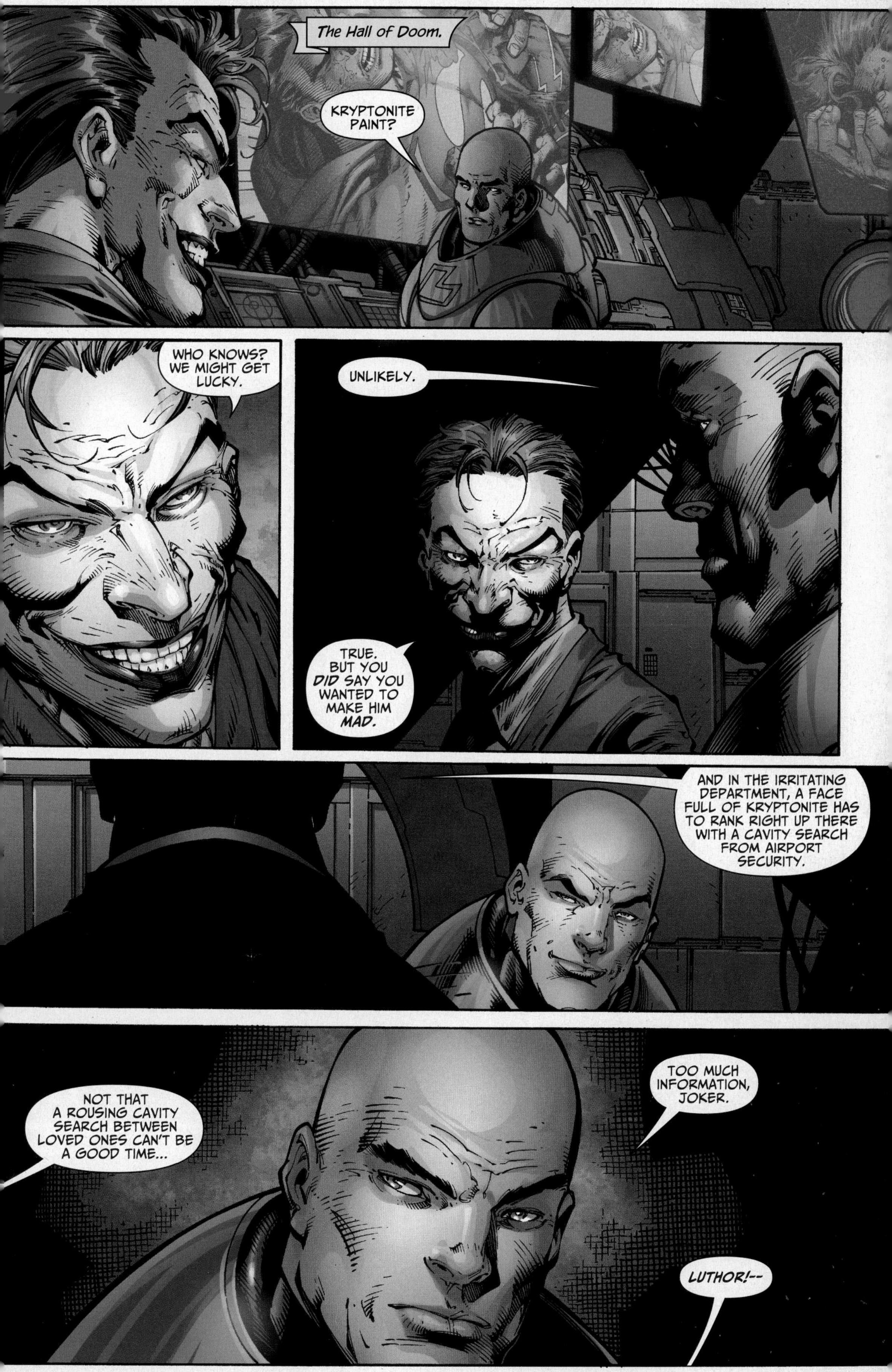
The Hall of Doom.
KRYPTONITE PAINT?
WHO KNOWS? WE MIGHT GET LUCKY.
UNLIKELY.
TRUE. BUT YOU *DID* SAY YOU WANTED TO MAKE HIM *MAD*.
AND IN THE IRRITATING DEPARTMENT, A FACE FULL OF KRYPTONITE HAS TO RANK RIGHT UP THERE WITH A CAVITY SEARCH FROM AIRPORT SECURITY.
NOT THAT A ROUSING CAVITY SEARCH BETWEEN LOVED ONES CAN'T BE A GOOD TIME...
TOO MUCH INFORMATION, JOKER.
LUTHOR!--

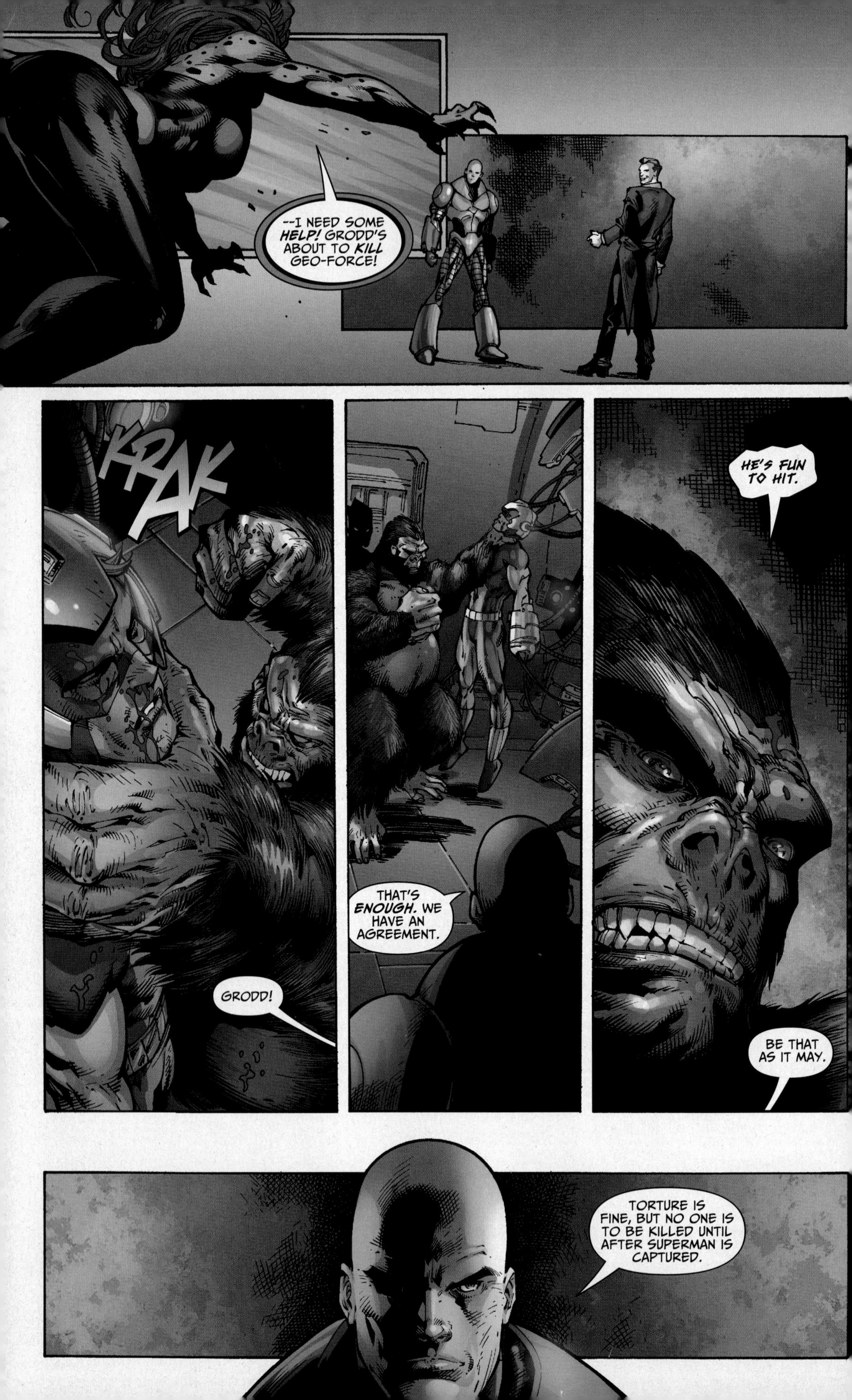
--I NEED SOME HELP! GRODD'S ABOUT TO KILL GEO-FORCE!
KRAK
GRODD!
THAT'S ENOUGH. WE HAVE AN AGREEMENT.
HE'S FUN TO HIT.
BE THAT AS IT MAY.
TORTURE IS FINE, BUT NO ONE IS TO BE KILLED UNTIL AFTER SUPERMAN IS CAPTURED.

YOU'RE THE BOSS, FOR NOW.

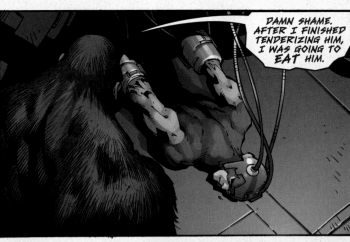

DAMN SHAME. AFTER I FINISHED TENDERIZING HIM, I WAS GOING TO *EAT* HIM.

HAAA-HA-HA-HA-HA! THAT WOULD HAVE BEEN SOMETHING TO SEE!

I APPRECIATE YOUR PATIENCE, GRODD.

THE FILMS WE'RE MAKING OF THEIR HUMILIATION AND DEFEAT ARE INSTRUMENTAL TO OUR LONG-RANGE GOALS.

IN ANY EVENT, IF I KNOW SUPERMAN, NONE OF US WILL HAVE TO WAIT FOR VERY LONG.

JUSTICE LEAGUE AMERICA

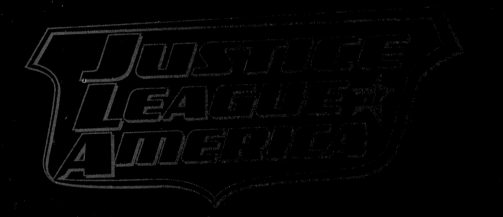

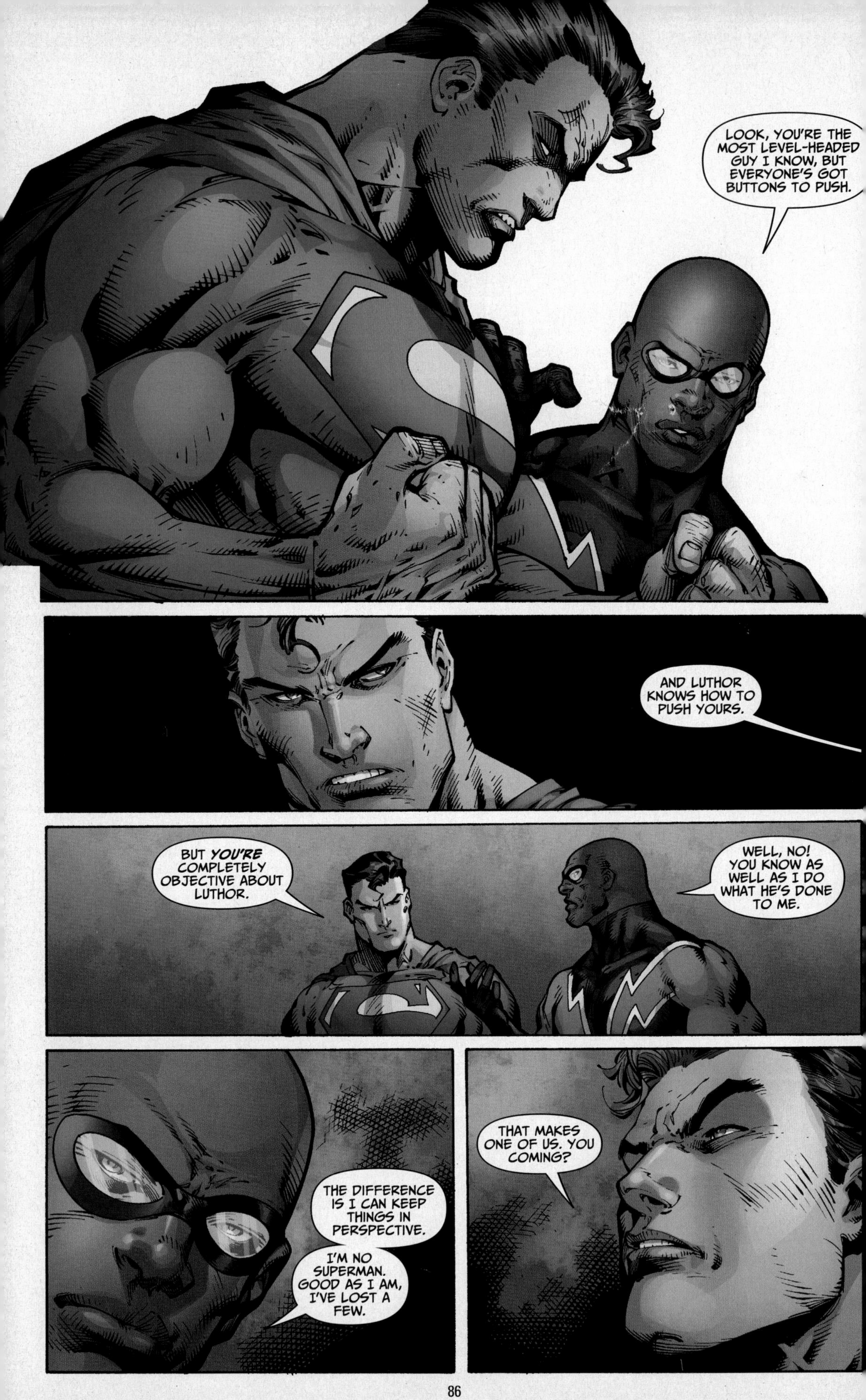
LOOK, YOU'RE THE MOST LEVEL-HEADED GUY I KNOW, BUT EVERYONE'S GOT BUTTONS TO PUSH.
AND LUTHOR KNOWS HOW TO PUSH YOURS.
BUT *YOU'RE* COMPLETELY OBJECTIVE ABOUT LUTHOR.
WELL, NO! YOU KNOW AS WELL AS I DO WHAT HE'S DONE TO ME.
THE DIFFERENCE IS I CAN KEEP THINGS IN PERSPECTIVE.
I'M NO SUPERMAN. GOOD AS I AM, I'VE LOST A FEW.
THAT MAKES ONE OF US. YOU COMING?

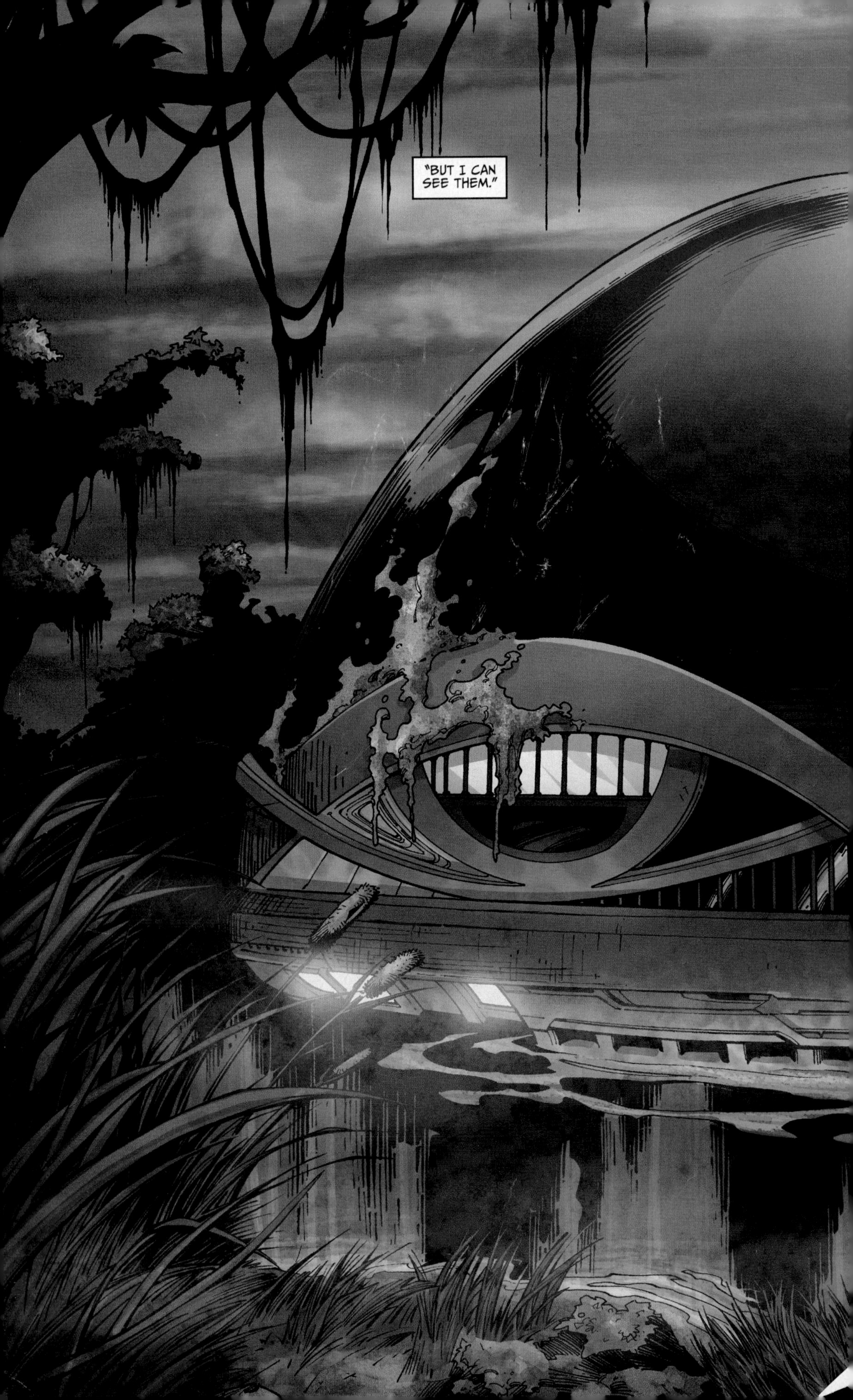
"BUT I CAN SEE THEM."

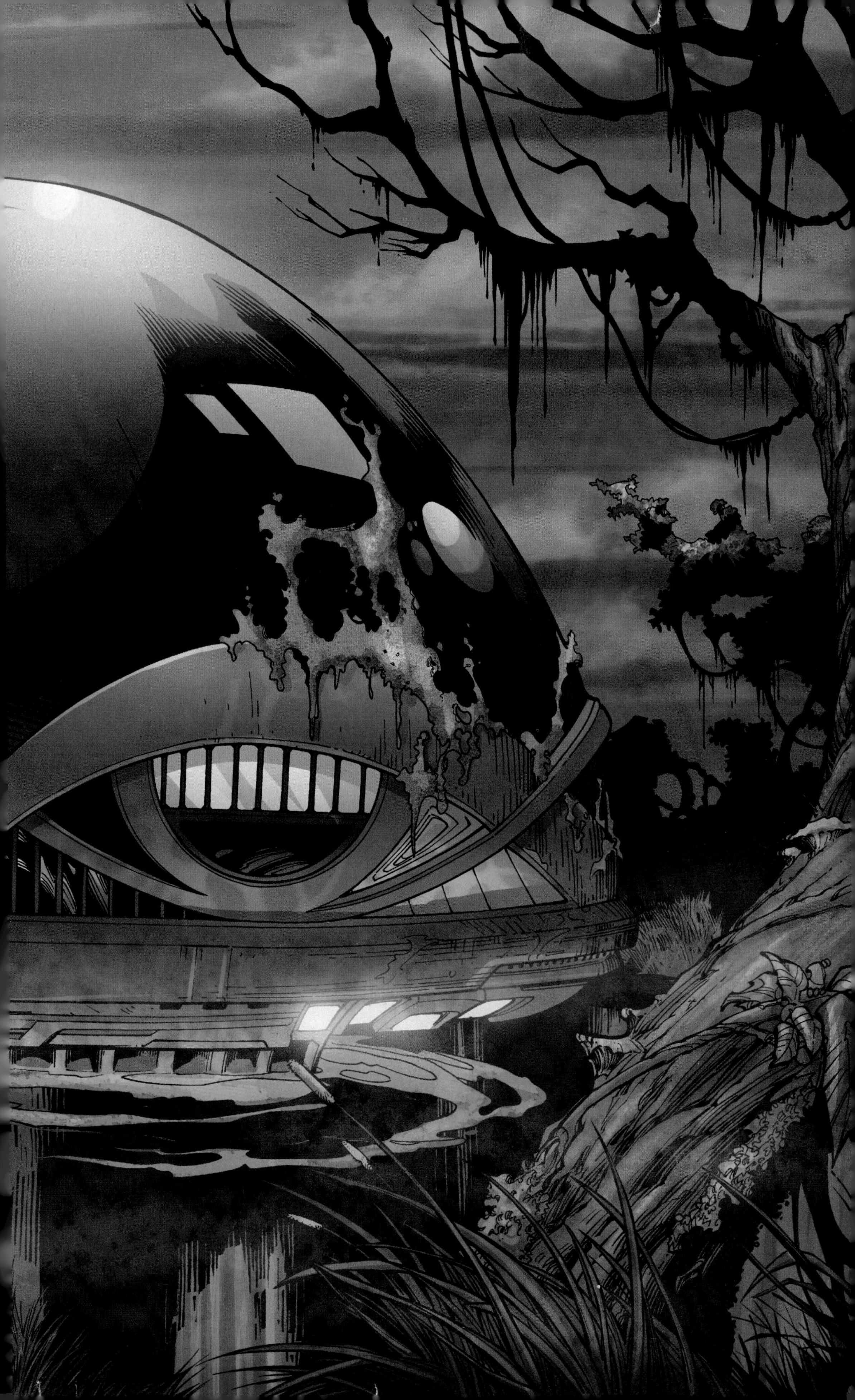

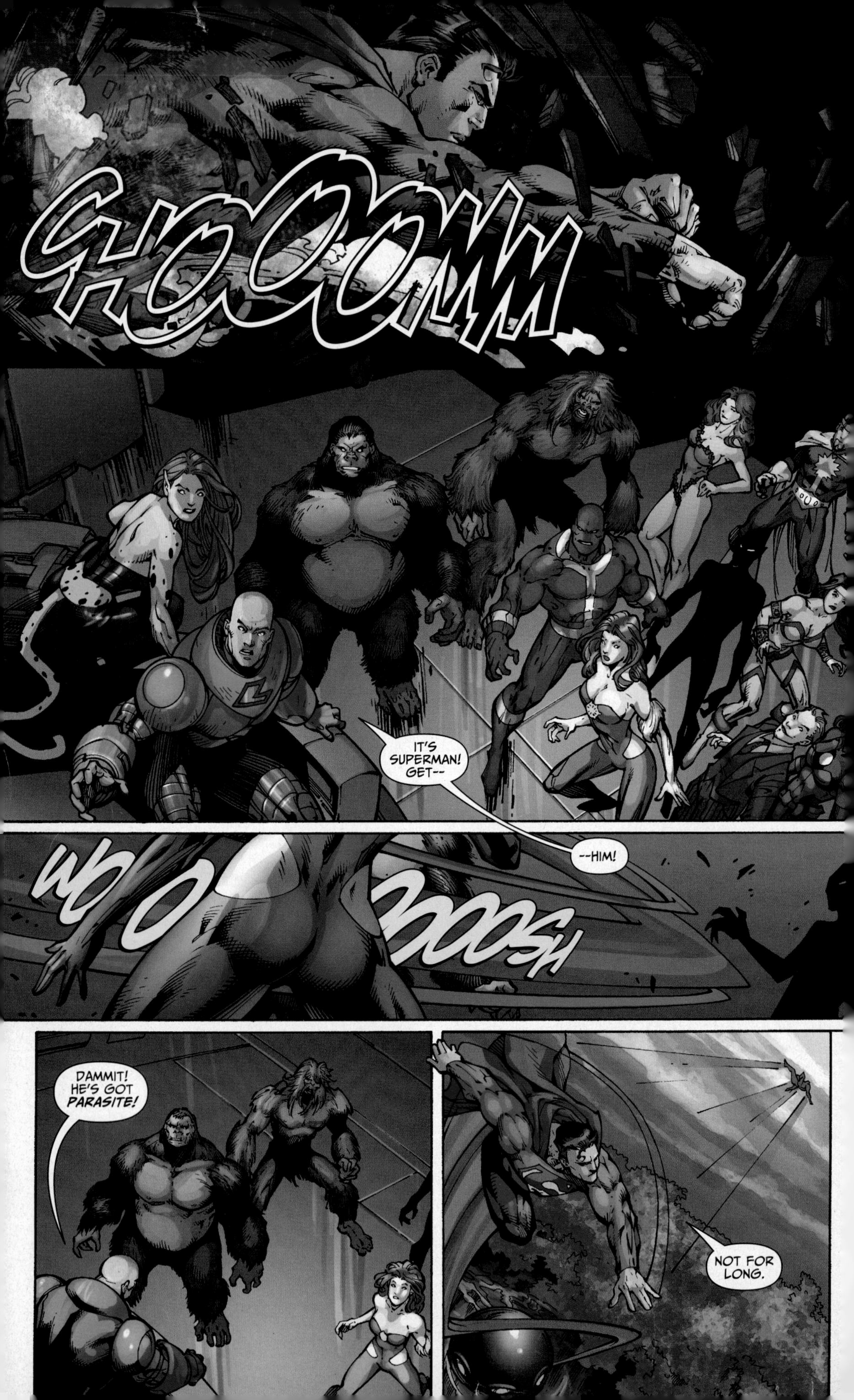
CHOOOMM
IT'S SUPERMAN! GET--
--HIM!
WHOOOOOOSH
DAMMIT! HE'S GOT *PARASITE!*
NOT FOR LONG.

PROTECT THE PRISONERS, HE'LL BE COMING AFTER THEM.

AHHHHHH!

IT *LOOKS* A LOT WORSE THAN IT ACTUALLY IS.

GHAKK

HE'S JUST A DECOY, KEEP YOUR EYES OUT FOR SUPERMAN!

ZZZ ZZZ

OH, NOW I'M JUST A *DECOY*...

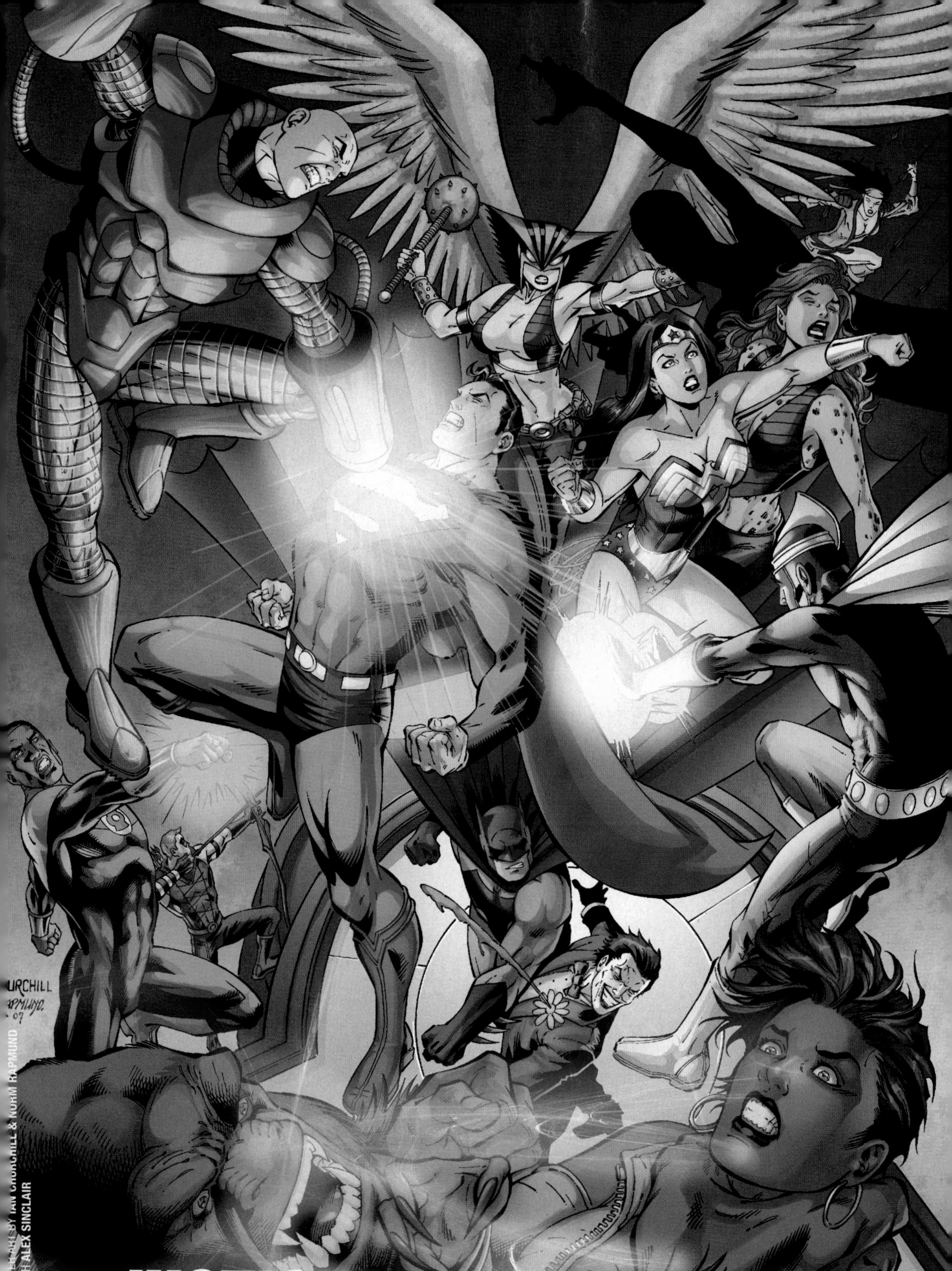

COVER ART BY IAN CHURCHILL & NORM RAPMUND
WITH ALEX SINCLAIR

JUSTICE LEAGUE OF AMERICA

CHAPTER FOUR

"I have to admit. This *looks* pretty bad."

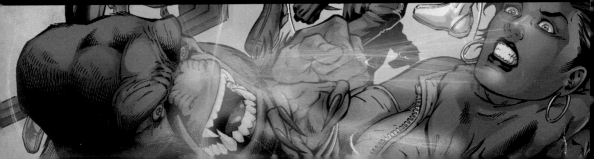

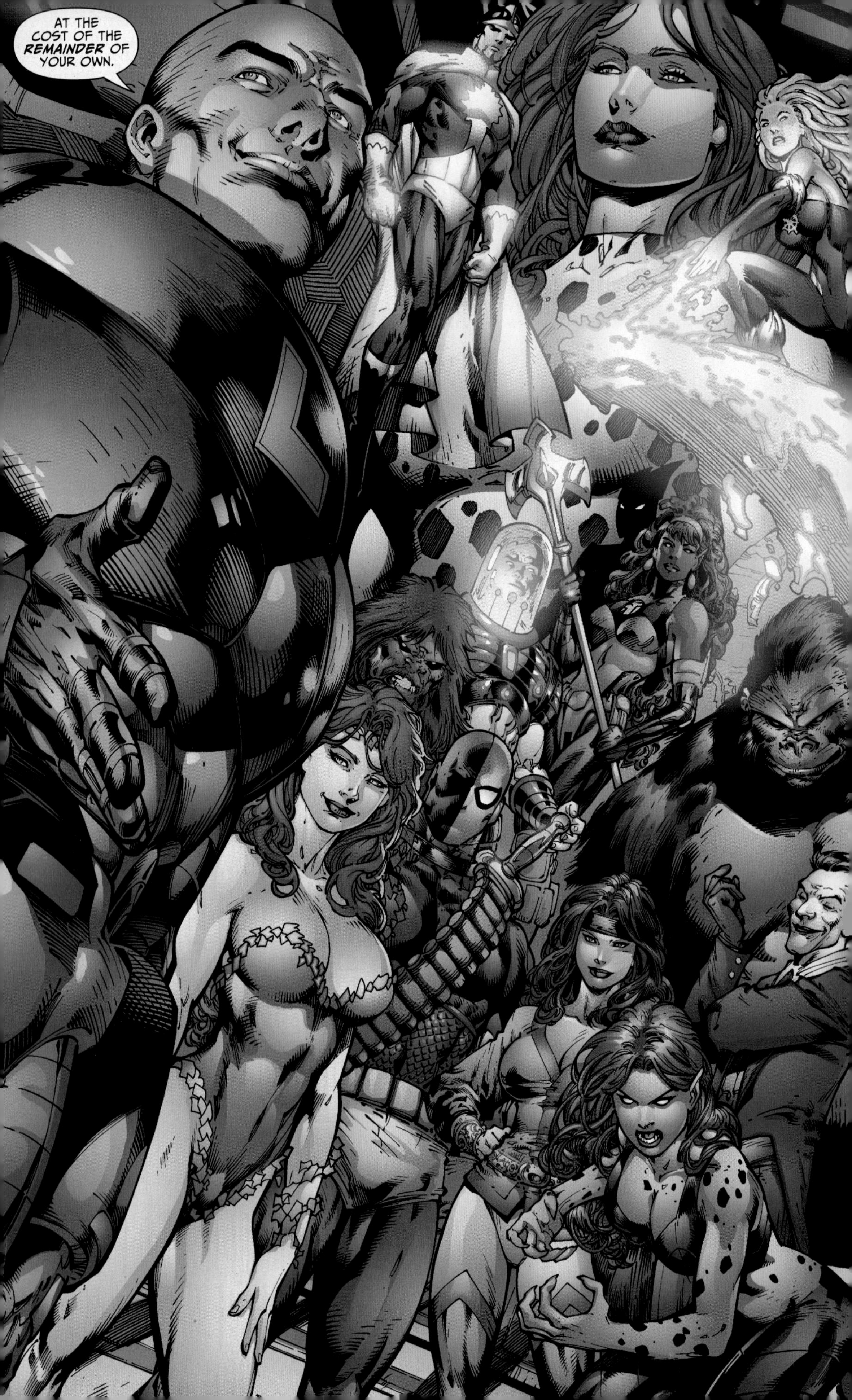
AT THE COST OF THE ***REMAINDER*** OF YOUR OWN.

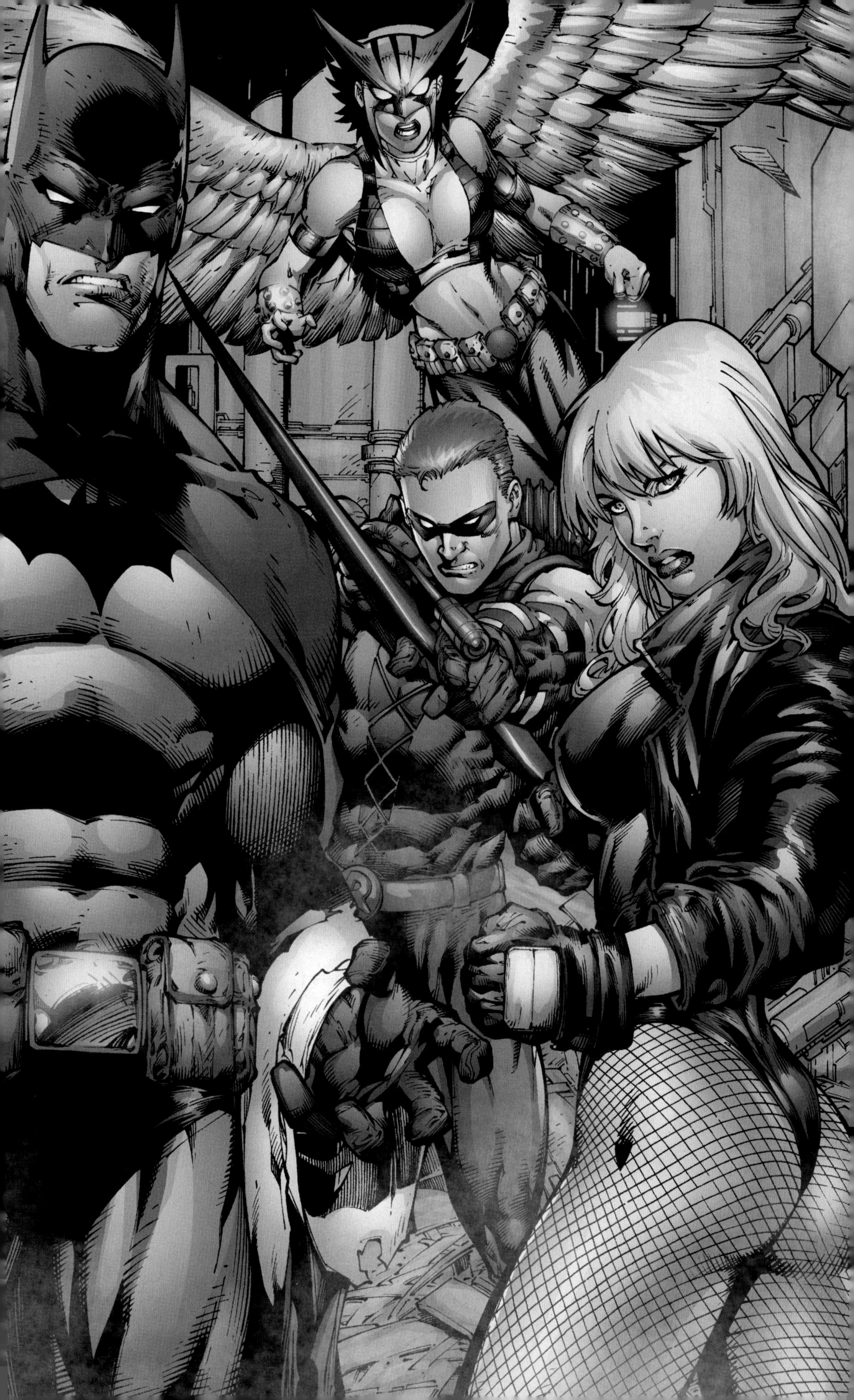

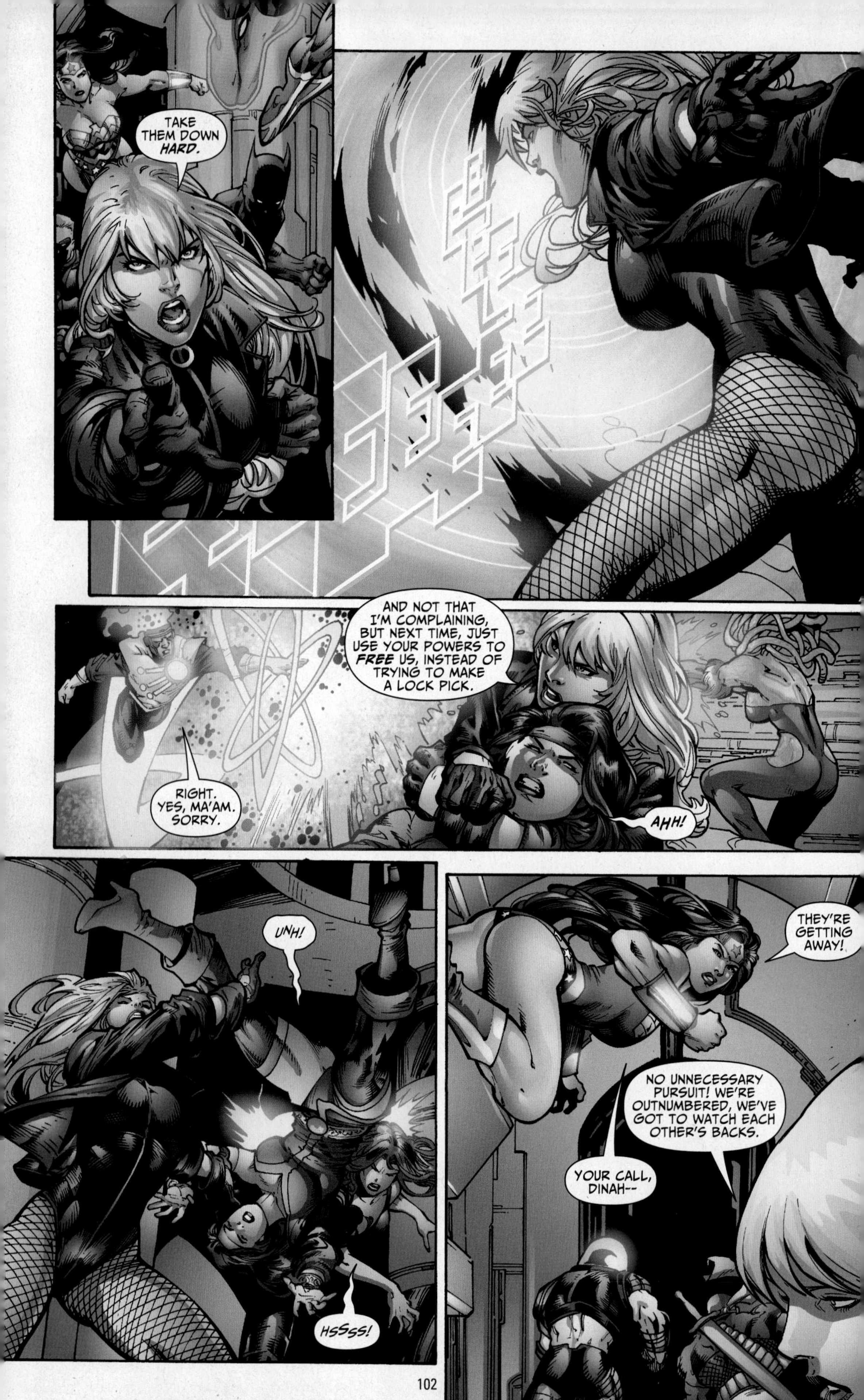
TAKE THEM DOWN *HARD*.
AND NOT THAT I'M COMPLAINING, BUT NEXT TIME, JUST USE YOUR POWERS TO *FREE* US, INSTEAD OF TRYING TO MAKE A LOCK PICK.
RIGHT. YES, MA'AM. SORRY.
AHH!
UNH!
HSSSS!
THEY'RE GETTING AWAY!
NO UNNECESSARY PURSUIT! WE'RE OUTNUMBERED, WE'VE GOT TO WATCH EACH OTHER'S BACKS.
YOUR CALL, DINAH--

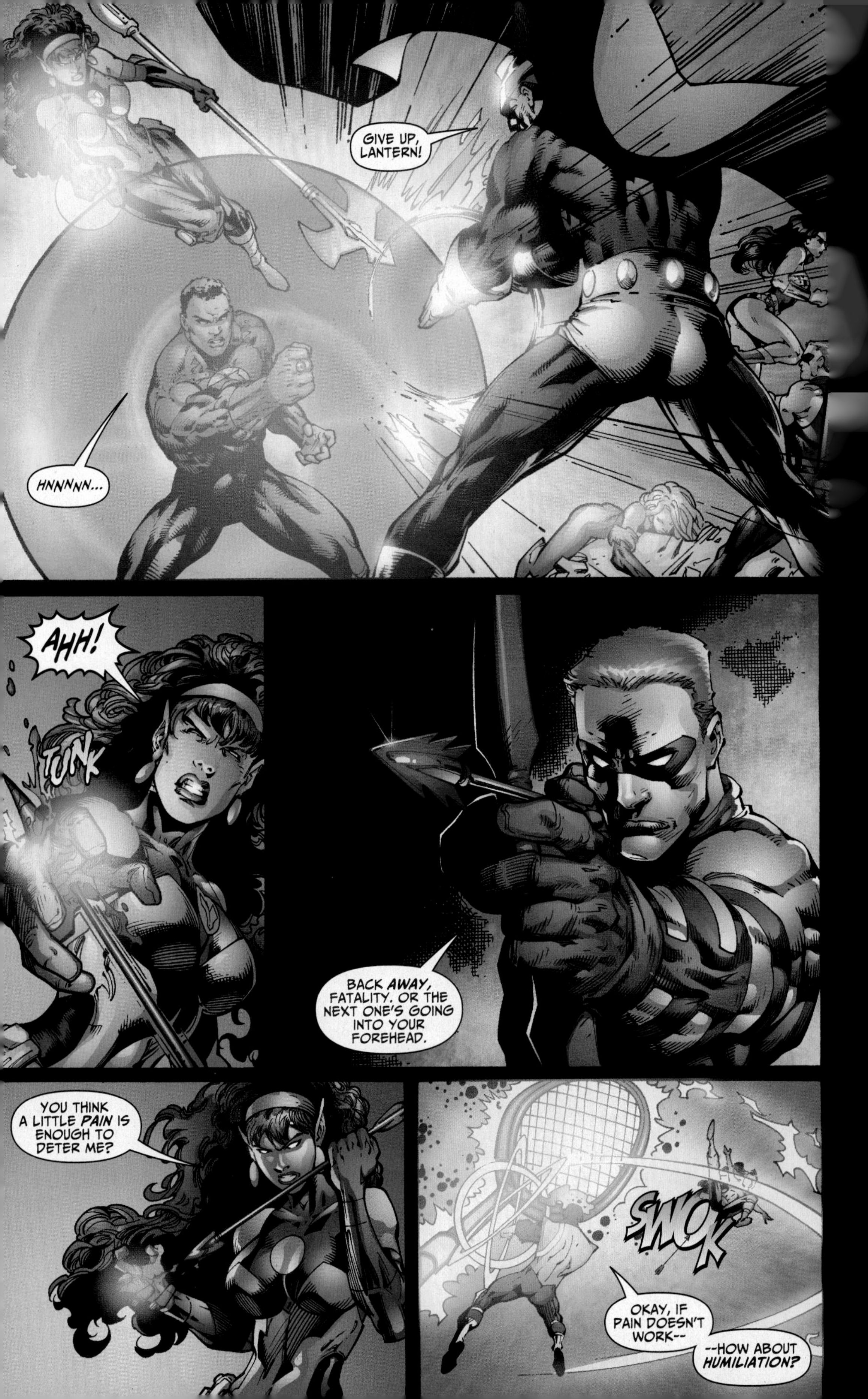
GIVE UP, LANTERN!
HNNNNN...
AHH!
TUNK
BACK AWAY, FATALITY. OR THE NEXT ONE'S GOING INTO YOUR FOREHEAD.
YOU THINK A LITTLE PAIN IS ENOUGH TO DETER ME?
SWOK
OKAY, IF PAIN DOESN'T WORK--
--HOW ABOUT HUMILIATION?

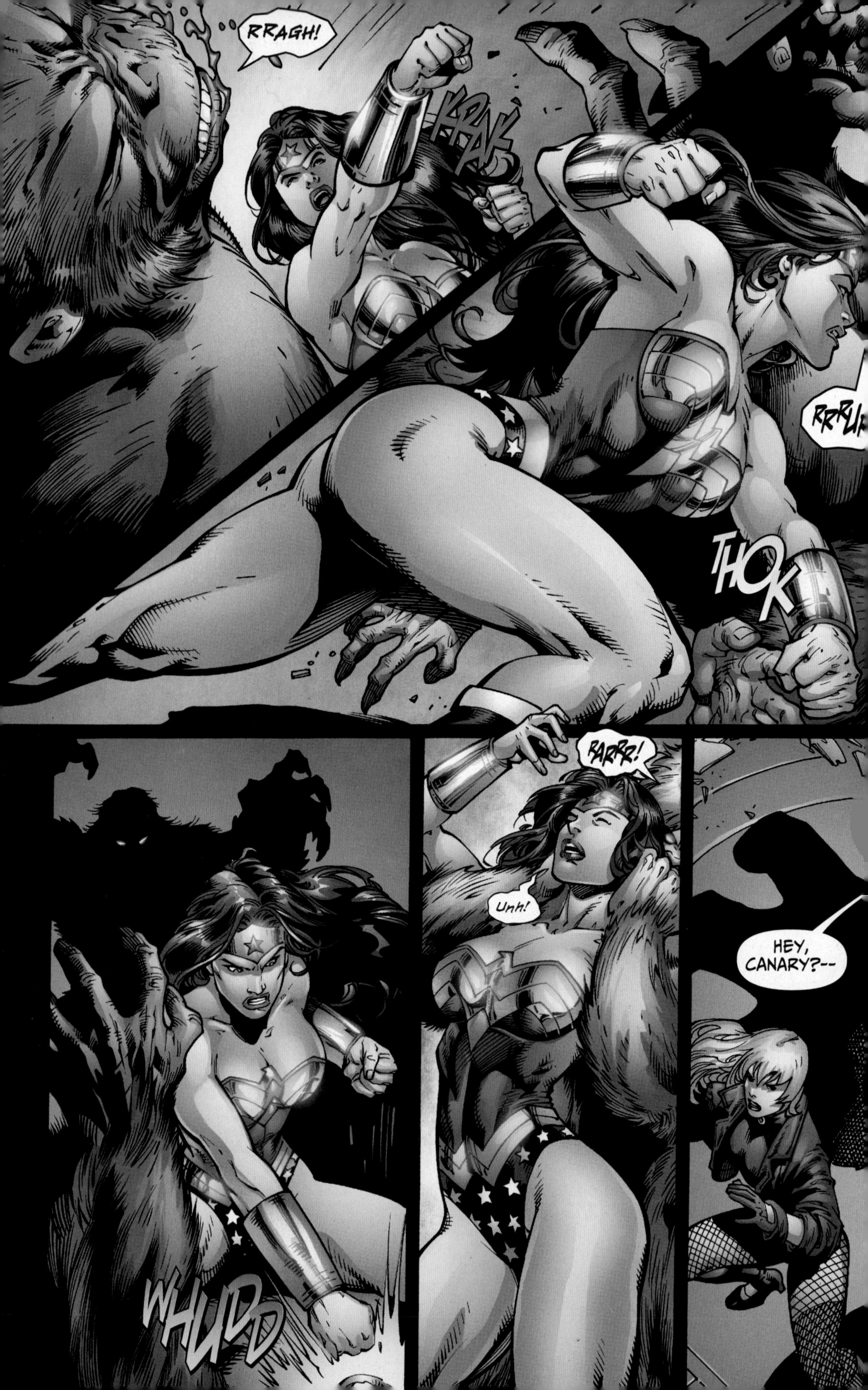
RRAGH!
KRAK
THOK
WHUDD
RARRR!
Unh!
HEY, CANARY?--

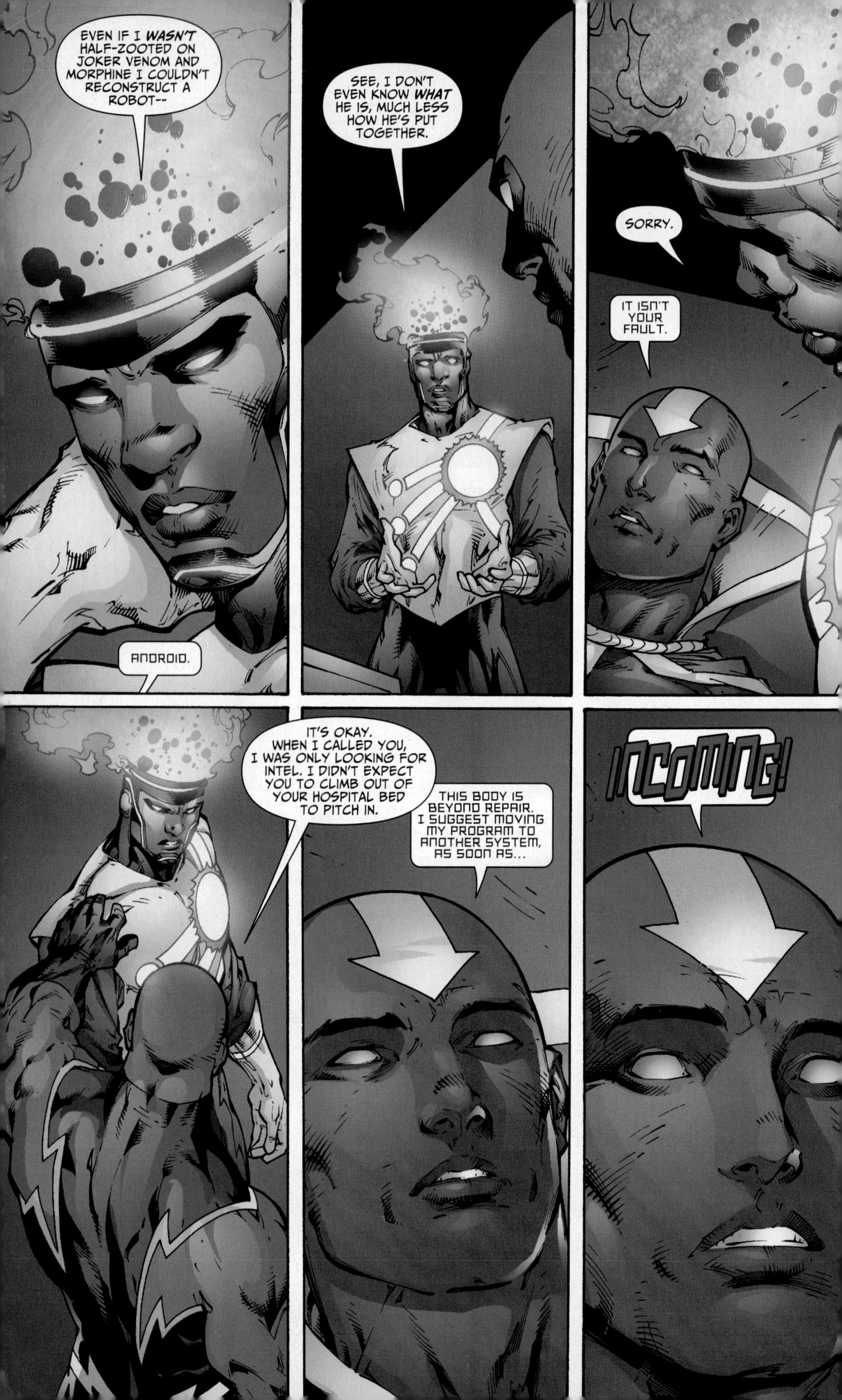
EVEN IF I WASN'T HALF-ZOOTED ON JOKER VENOM AND MORPHINE I COULDN'T RECONSTRUCT A ROBOT--
ANDROID.
SEE, I DON'T EVEN KNOW WHAT HE IS, MUCH LESS HOW HE'S PUT TOGETHER.
SORRY.
IT ISN'T YOUR FAULT.
IT'S OKAY. WHEN I CALLED YOU, I WAS ONLY LOOKING FOR INTEL. I DIDN'T EXPECT YOU TO CLIMB OUT OF YOUR HOSPITAL BED TO PITCH IN.
THIS BODY IS BEYOND REPAIR. I SUGGEST MOVING MY PROGRAM TO ANOTHER SYSTEM, AS SOON AS...
INCOMING!

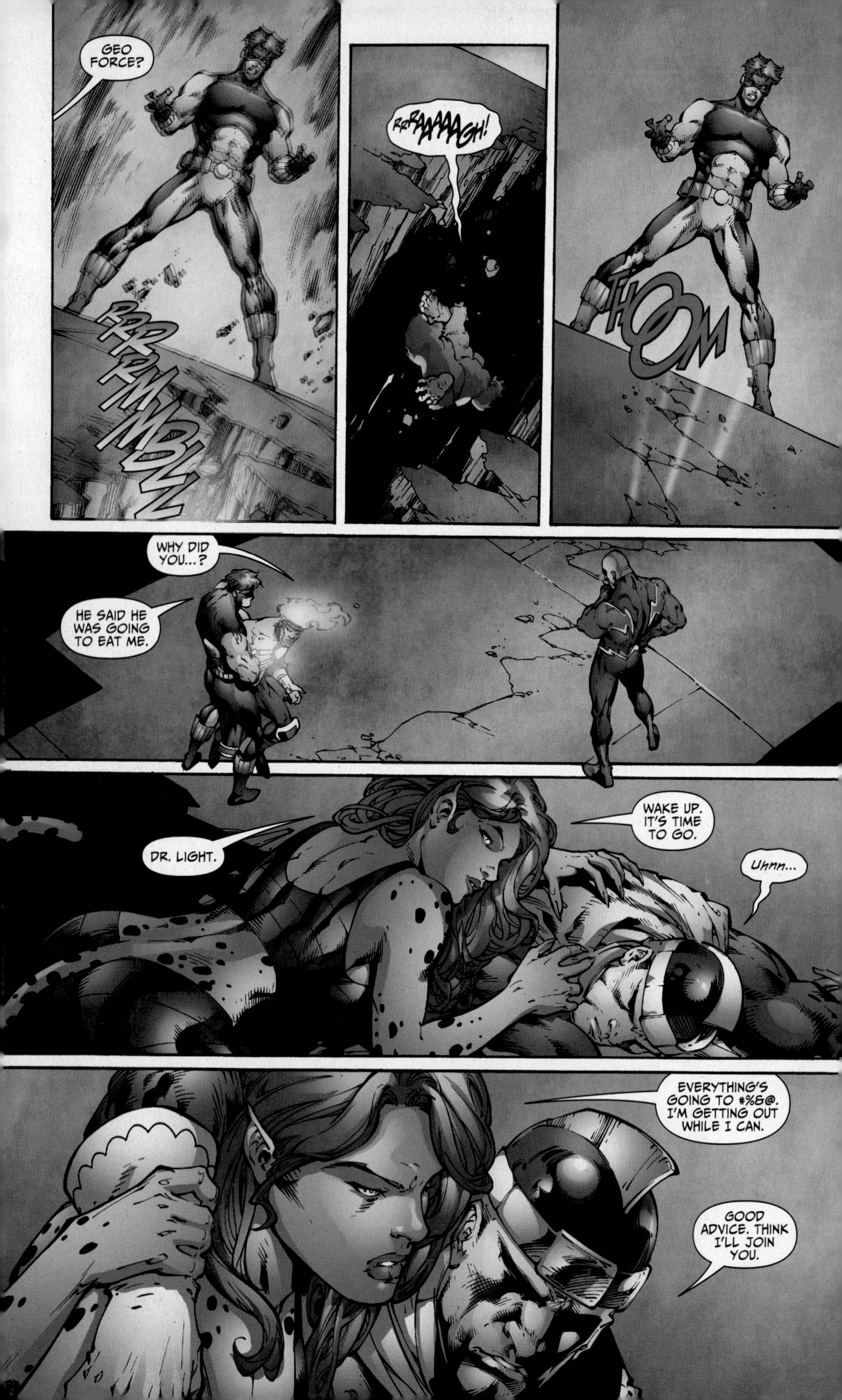
GEO FORCE?
RRRRMMBLLL
RRRAAAAAGH!
THOOM
WHY DID YOU...?
HE SAID HE WAS GOING TO EAT ME.
DR. LIGHT.
WAKE UP. IT'S TIME TO GO.
Unnn...
EVERYTHING'S GOING TO #%&@. I'M GETTING OUT WHILE I CAN.
GOOD ADVICE. THINK I'LL JOIN YOU.

AND *YOU'RE* GOING TO STOP ME?

NO. NOT THIS TIME.

FZAM

AHH!

LUTHOR!

YOU AND ME. RIGHT HERE, RIGHT NOW.

IT WOULD BE MY *PLEASURE*, KRYPTONIAN.

ONE SECOND, LEX--

--IF IT'S GOING TO BE A FAIR FIGHT, THOSE KRYPTONITE GAUNTLETS HAVE TO GO.

FZAM

Unph!

STOP SQUIRMING. YOU'RE NOT GETTING LOOSE UNTIL WE FEEL LIKE IT.

NOW THEN, I THINK SOMEBODY WAS SUPPOSED TO BE GETTING READY FOR A *WEDDING* IN A FEW HOURS?

YEAH. I'VE *REALLY* GOT TO GET GOING. SEE YOU ALL THERE.

NICE WORK TODAY. IF YOU EVER NEED THE LEAGUE'S HELP ON ANYTHING, JUST ASK.

I WAS THINKING MORE ALONG THE LINES OF HIM *JOINING* THE TEAM.

OH. *Uh,* I'M *HONORED,* OF COURSE, BUT I REALLY DON' HAVE TIME RIGHT NOW TO--

THAT WASN'T AN *OFFER,* SON. IT'S THE WAY IT'S GOING TO BE. YOU'RE TOO POWERFUL TO BE OUT THERE UNSUPERVISED.

AND THE BAT-GOD HAS SPOKEN.

I AGREE WITH HIM, THOUGH.

THEN IT'S SETTLED. WELCOME TO THE JUSTICE LEAGUE.

JUSTICE LEAGUE AMERICA

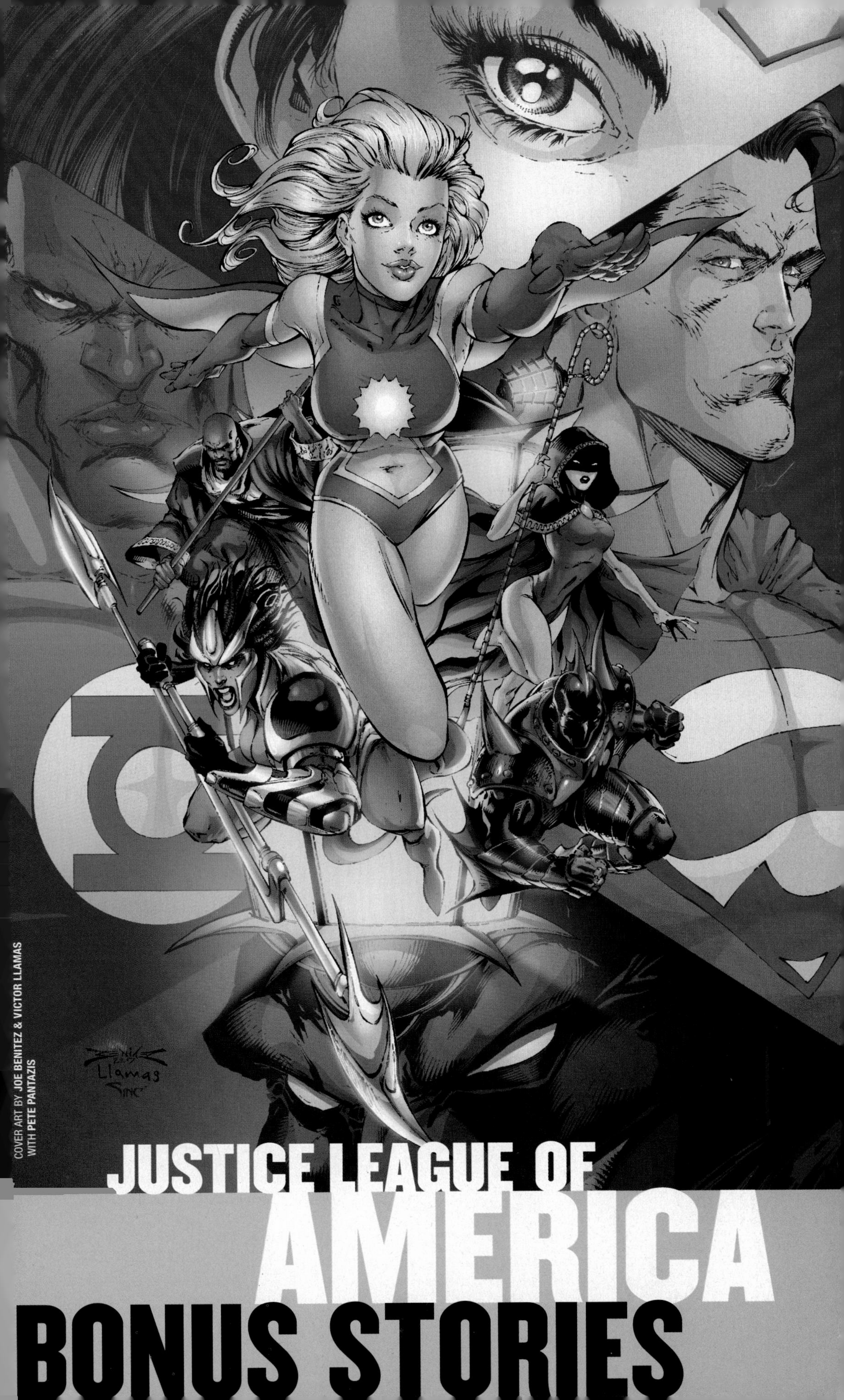

COVER ART BY JOE BENITEZ & VICTOR LLAMAS
WITH PETE PANTAZIS

JUSTICE LEAGUE OF AMERICA
BONUS STORIES

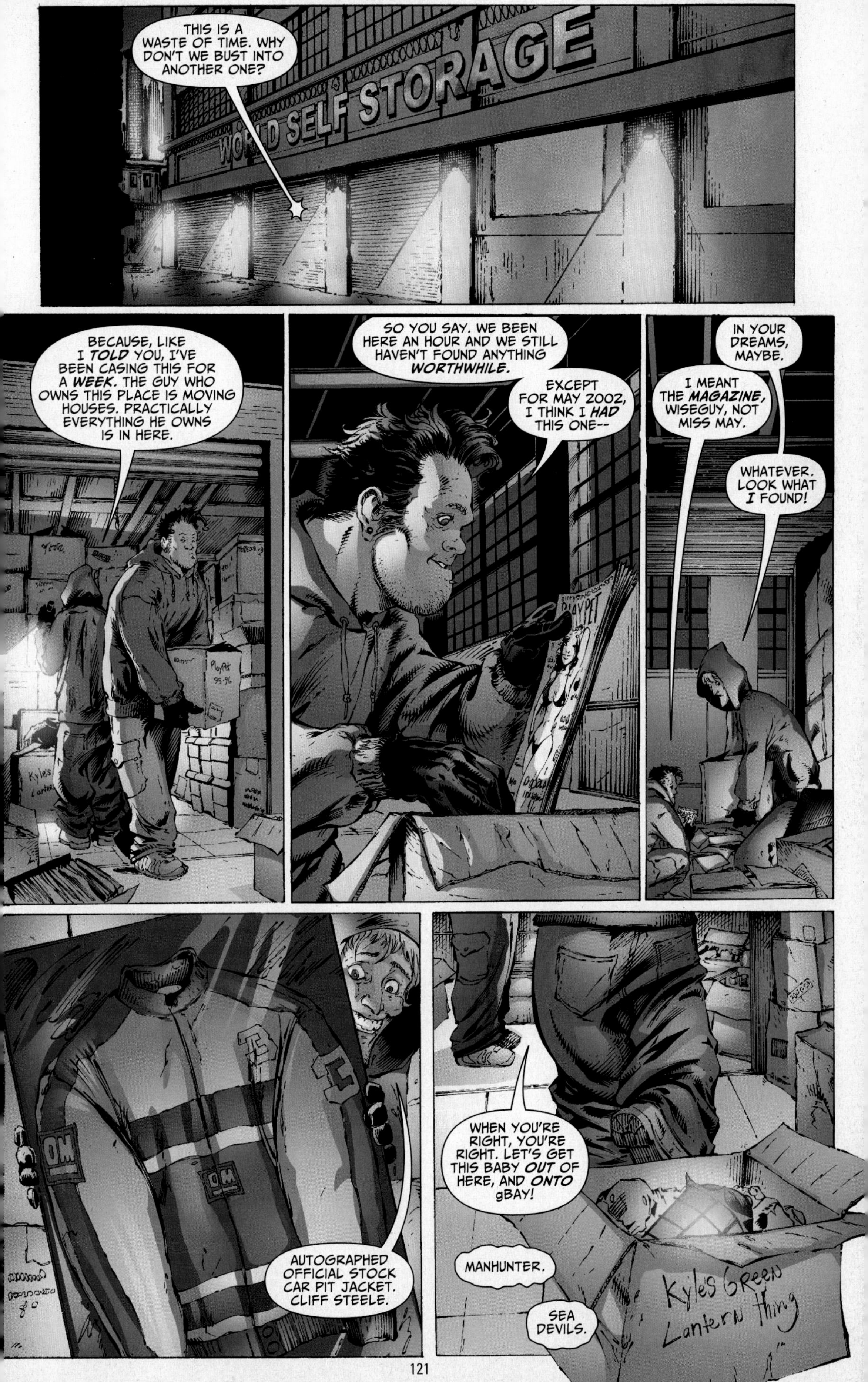
WORLD SELF STORAGE
THIS IS A WASTE OF TIME. WHY DON'T WE BUST INTO ANOTHER ONE?
BECAUSE, LIKE I TOLD YOU, I'VE BEEN CASING THIS FOR A WEEK. THE GUY WHO OWNS THIS PLACE IS MOVING HOUSES. PRACTICALLY EVERYTHING HE OWNS IS IN HERE.
SO YOU SAY. WE BEEN HERE AN HOUR AND WE STILL HAVEN'T FOUND ANYTHING WORTHWHILE.
EXCEPT FOR MAY 2002, I THINK I HAD THIS ONE--
IN YOUR DREAMS, MAYBE.
I MEANT THE MAGAZINE, WISEGUY, NOT MISS MAY.
WHATEVER. LOOK WHAT I FOUND!
AUTOGRAPHED OFFICIAL STOCK CAR PIT JACKET. CLIFF STEELE.
WHEN YOU'RE RIGHT, YOU'RE RIGHT. LET'S GET THIS BABY OUT OF HERE, AND ONTO gBAY!
MANHUNTER.
SEA DEVILS.
Kyle's Green Lantern thing

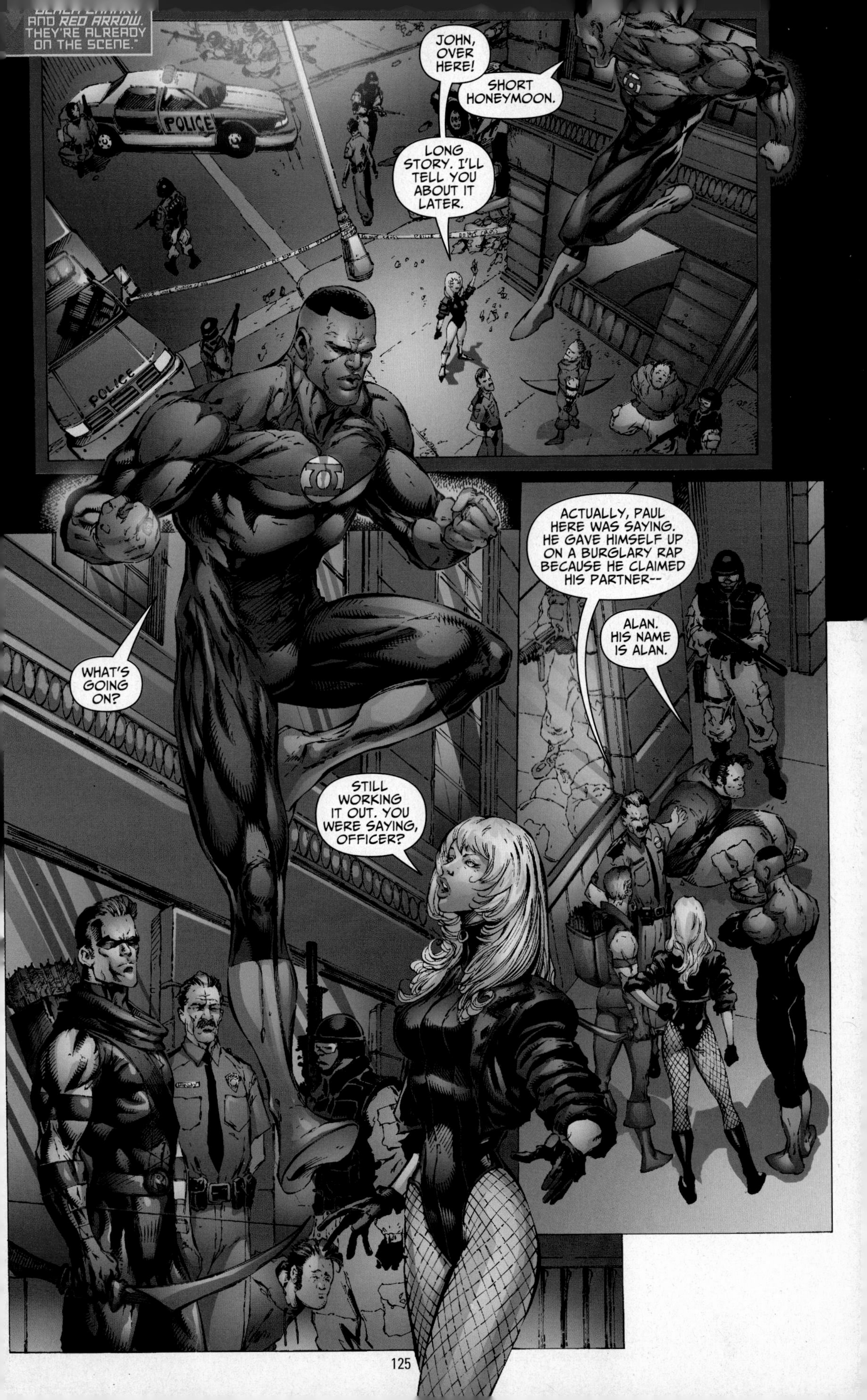
AND RED ARROW. THEY'RE ALREADY ON THE SCENE."
JOHN, OVER HERE!
SHORT HONEYMOON.
LONG STORY. I'LL TELL YOU ABOUT IT LATER.
POLICE
POLICE
WHAT'S GOING ON?
STILL WORKING IT OUT. YOU WERE SAYING, OFFICER?
ACTUALLY, PAUL HERE WAS SAYING. HE GAVE HIMSELF UP ON A BURGLARY RAP BECAUSE HE CLAIMED HIS PARTNER--
ALAN. HIS NAME IS ALAN.

AND WE APPRECIATE IT, BUT THAT WASN'T THE REASON WE CONTACTED YOU. NOT AT FIRST.

I DON'T FOLLOW.

WE CALLED YOU BEFORE WE EVEN COMPLETELY *BELIEVED* THE STORY ABOUT THE SUPER-VILLAIN. IT WAS THE *LOCATION*.

THE STORAGE UNIT THEY BROKE INTO IS LEASED BY *GUY GARDNER*.

HE'S ONE OF YOURS, RIGHT?

RED ARROW AND I WILL CHECK IT OUT. JOHN, GET IN TOUCH WITH GUY, SEE IF THERE'S ANY WAY THIS COULD REALLY BE HIS LANTERN.

ON IT.

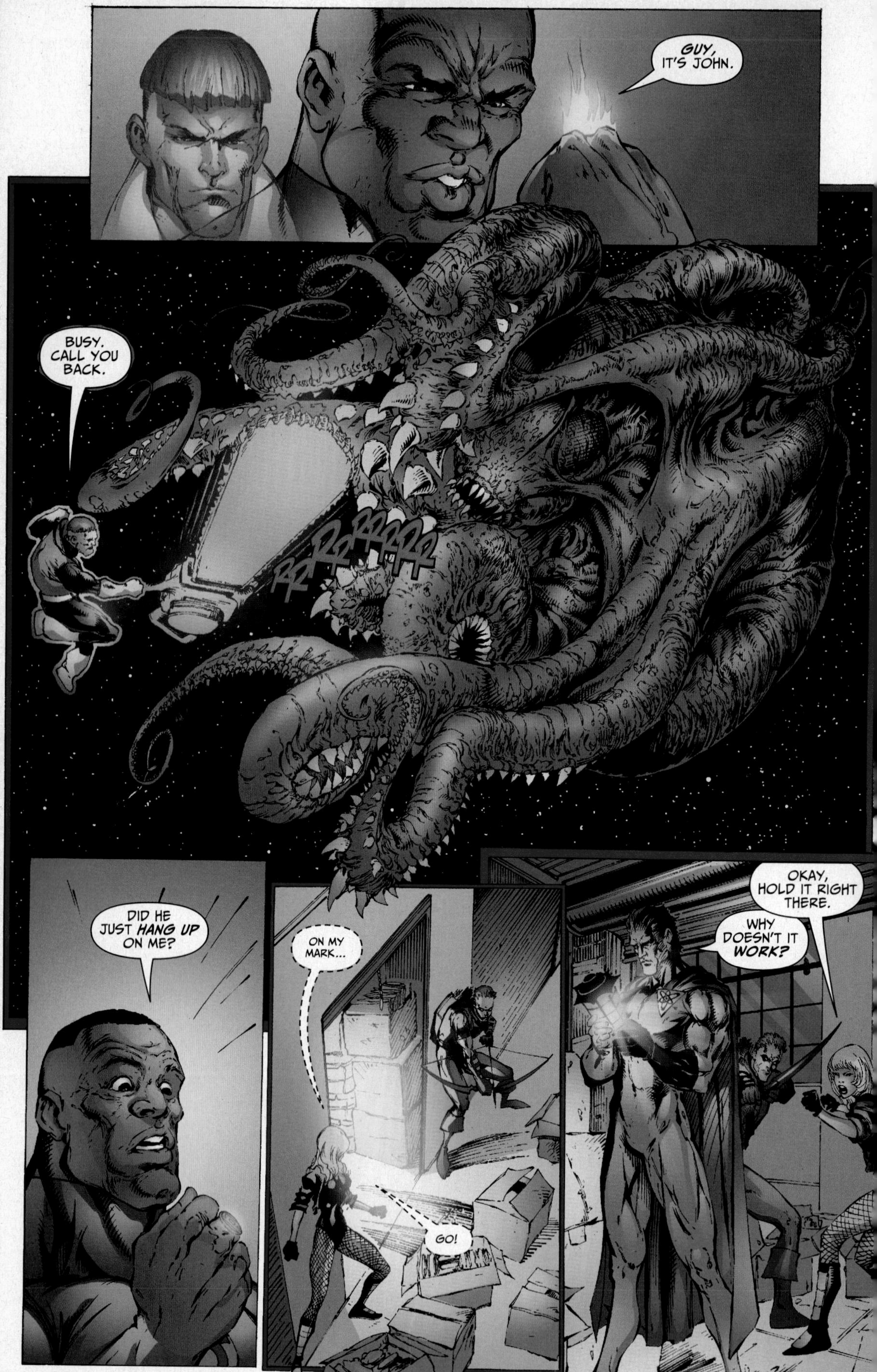
GUY, IT'S JOHN.
BUSY. CALL YOU BACK.
RRRRRRRRRR
DID HE JUST HANG UP ON ME?
ON MY MARK...
GO!
OKAY, HOLD IT RIGHT THERE.
WHY DOESN'T IT WORK?

Panel 1: I'M IN *HERE*, JOHN!

JUST A SECOND...

Panel 2: THANKS.

YOUR CANARY CRY NOT WORKING?

IT WORKS FINE, BUT I MIGHT *NEED* IT IF ROY CAN'T HANDLE THE GUY UPSTAIRS.

Panel 3: YOU TALK TO GUY?

TRIED TO, HE'S A LITTLE BUSY.

YOU GOTTA BE *KIDDING* ME. GET *HIM*.

Panel 4: GUY!

HANH!

WHAT THE *HELL* IS YOUR POWER BATTERY DOING IN YOUR STORAGE UNIT? SOMEBODY'S TRYING TO STEAL IT.

MY POWER BATTERY AIN'T IN STORAGE, IT'S--

ARE YOU TALKING ABOUT THAT CHEAP PAPER LANTERN THAT KYLE GAVE ME?

IT'S NOT YOUR POWER BATTERY?

NAH, IT'S SOME KIND OF TRANSDIMENSIONAL INTER-THINGY. I'M SUPPOSED TO HOLD IT UNTIL KYLE COMES BACK. MY STORAGE ISN'T GOOD?

TELL KYLE WE'LL KEEP IT IN THE HALL OF JUSTICE.

DID HE HAPPEN TO MENTION HOW IT WORKS?

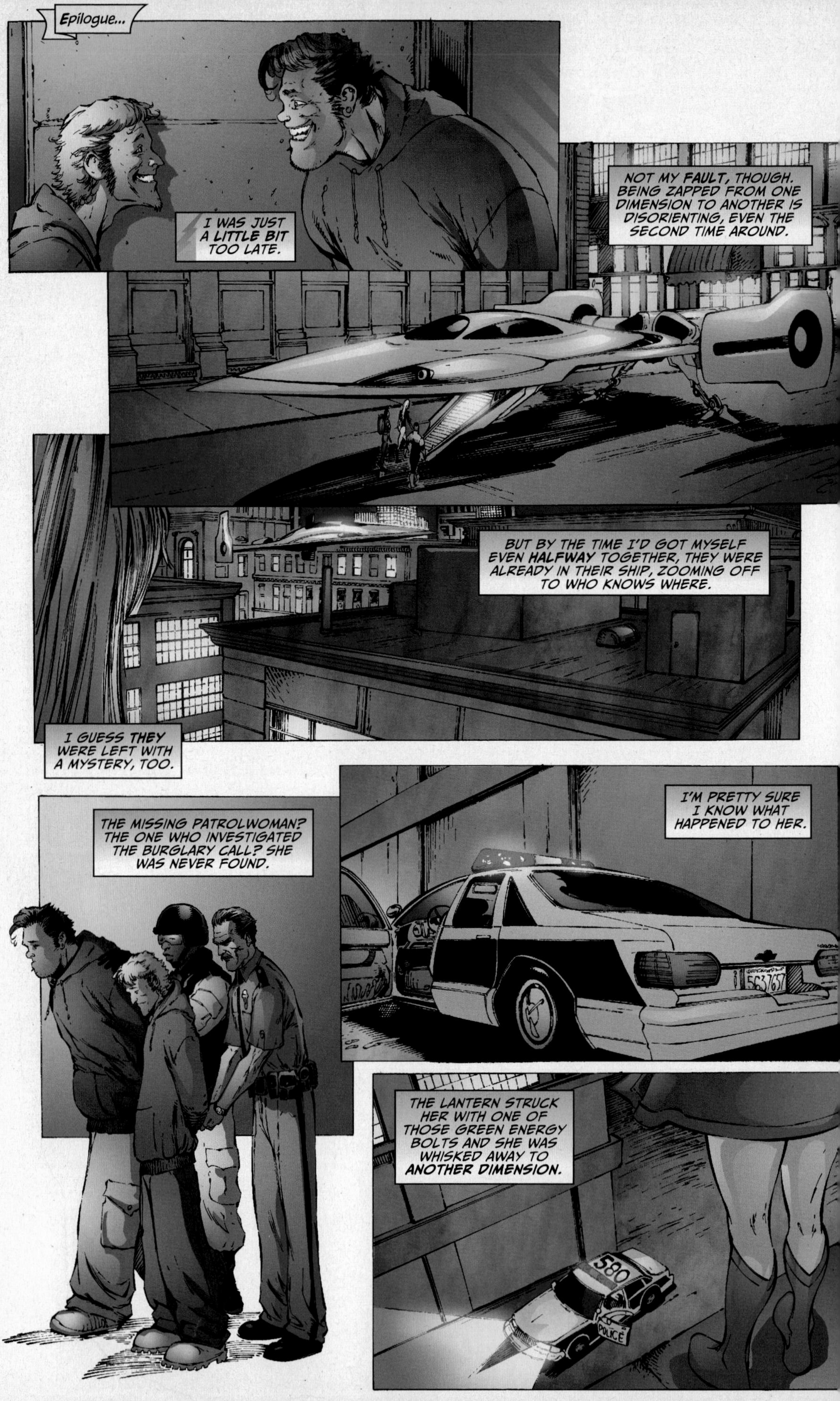
Epilogue...
I WAS JUST A LITTLE BIT TOO LATE.
NOT MY FAULT, THOUGH. BEING ZAPPED FROM ONE DIMENSION TO ANOTHER IS DISORIENTING, EVEN THE SECOND TIME AROUND.
BUT BY THE TIME I'D GOT MYSELF EVEN HALFWAY TOGETHER, THEY WERE ALREADY IN THEIR SHIP, ZOOMING OFF TO WHO KNOWS WHERE.
I GUESS THEY WERE LEFT WITH A MYSTERY, TOO.
THE MISSING PATROLWOMAN? THE ONE WHO INVESTIGATED THE BURGLARY CALL? SHE WAS NEVER FOUND.
I'M PRETTY SURE I KNOW WHAT HAPPENED TO HER.
THE LANTERN STRUCK HER WITH ONE OF THOSE GREEN ENERGY BOLTS AND SHE WAS WHISKED AWAY TO ANOTHER DIMENSION.
580
POLICE

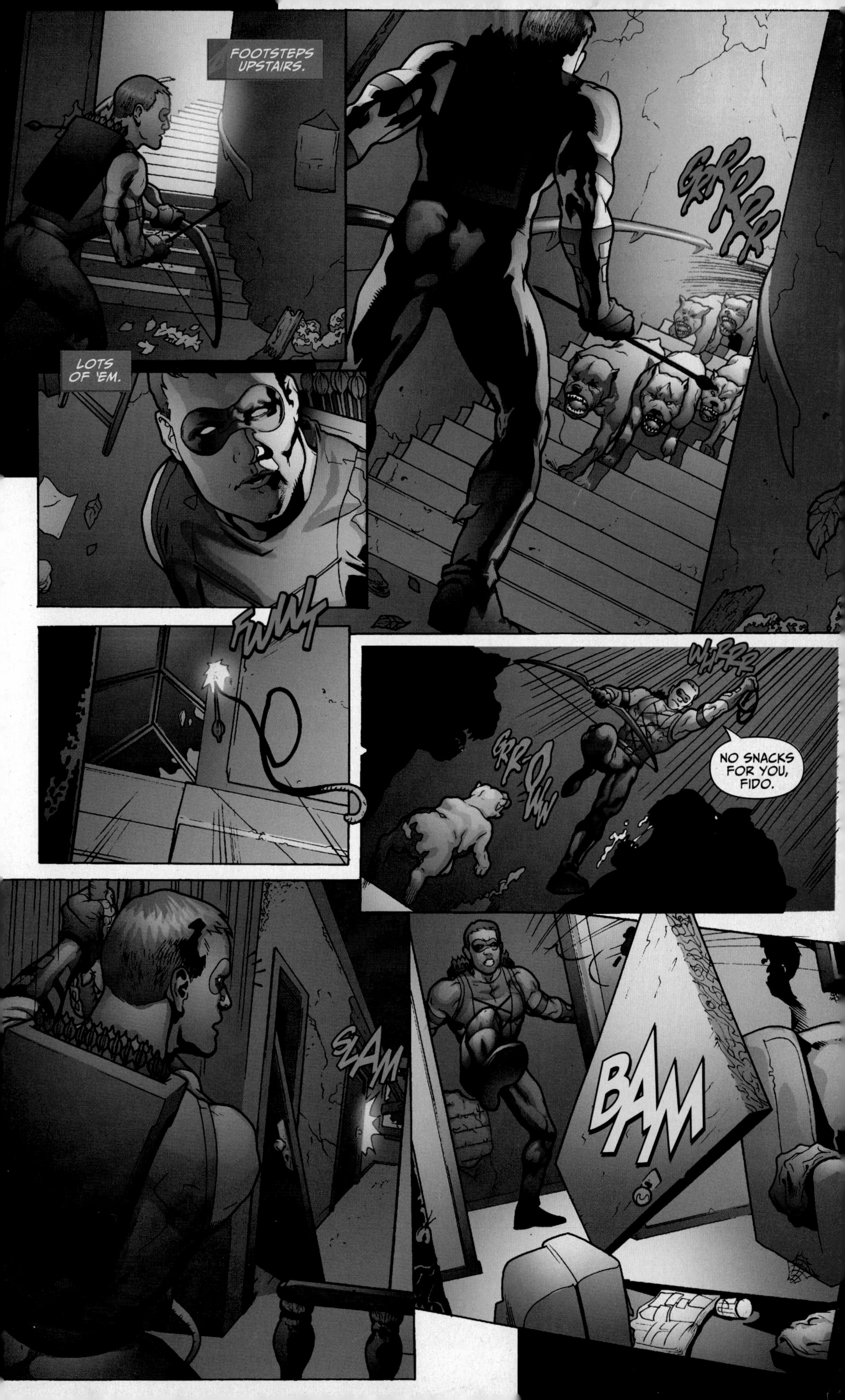
FOOTSTEPS UPSTAIRS.
GRRRRR
LOTS OF 'EM.
FWWF
WHRRR
GRR-OWW
NO SNACKS FOR YOU, FIDO.
SLAM
BAM

IT SURE AIN'T THE PALACE. REMINDS ME OF MY SICK DAYS.

THE TITANS?

THE FIRE ESCAPE!

CRAAACH!T

GAHH!

OKAY, THIS IS GETTIN' PERSONAL.

I'LL SAY ONE THING, THE GUY CAN LEAP.

OKAY, TH! PIGEON GE CAGED.

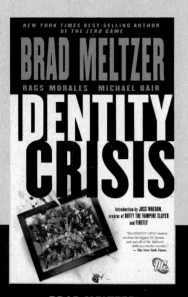